The Francis Factor
and the People of God

Also by Gerald A. Arbuckle, SM

The Chatham Islands in Perspective

Strategies for Growth in Religious Life

Out of Chaos*

Earthing the Gospel*

Grieving for Changes

Refounding the Church*

From Chaos to Mission

Healthcare Ministry*

Dealing with Bullies

Confronting the Demon

Violence, Society and the Church

Crafting Catholic Identity in Postmodern Australia

A 'Preferential Option for the Poor'

Laughing with God

Culture, Inculturation, and Theologians

Humanizing Healthcare Reforms

Catholic Identity or Identities?**

*Catholic Press Award
**Association of Catholic Publishers Award

The Francis Factor and the People of God

New Life for the Church

Gerald A. Arbuckle, SM

ORBIS BOOKS
Maryknoll, New York 10545

ORBIS BOOKS
Maryknoll, New York 10545

Fathers and Brothers
MARYKNOLL.

Founded in 1970, Orbis Books endeavors to publish works that enlighten the mind, nourish the spirit, and challenge the conscience. The publishing arm of the Maryknoll Fathers and Brothers, Orbis seeks to explore the global dimensions of the Christian faith and mission, to invite dialogue with diverse cultures and religious traditions, and to serve the cause of reconciliation and peace. The books published reflect the views of their authors and do not represent the official position of the Maryknoll Society. To learn more about Maryknoll and Orbis Books, please visit our website at www.maryknollsociety.org.

Published by Orbis Books, Maryknoll, New York 10545-0302.

Manufactured in the United States of America.

Copy editing and typesetting by Joan Weber Laflamme.

Library of Congress Cataloging-in-Publication Data

Arbuckle, Gerald A.
   The Francis factor and the people of God : new life for the church / Gerald A. Arbuckle, S.M.
      pages cm
   Includes bibliographical references and index.
   ISBN 978-1-62698-125-6 (pbk.)
   1. Church renewal—Catholic Church. 2. Aging—Biblical teaching. 3. Aging—Religious aspects—Catholic Church. I. Title.
BX1746.A8225 2015
282.09'051—dc23

                                                      2014037603

To Rosemary and Terry Arbuckle,
Gillian Paterson and Margaret Zucker:
examples of youthfulness in aging

I offer particular thanks to Robert Ellsberg and Jim Keane for accepting on behalf of Orbis Books this book for publication; the community of Campion Hall, Oxford University, for providing me with a congenial atmosphere where most of the research for this book took place; my Marist superiors who so generously support my ministry of writing; and Margaret Zucker for offering wise comments on the text. These people, however, are in no way responsible for the book's inadequacies. The scriptural quotations are from the New Revised Standard Version.

Contents

Introduction

Our life is a journey, and when you stop moving, things go wrong.
—Pope Francis, Homily, March 14, 2013

Give sorrow words: the grief that does not speak
Whispers the o'er-fraught heart, and bids it break
—William Shakespeare, *Macbeth*

The management of change depends upon our ability to articulate the process of grieving [in mourning rituals]. . . . When loss cannot be articulated, its suppressed tensions will in the end prove more profoundly disruptive than the social conflicts which relieve them.
—Peter Marris, *Loss and Change*

This is a book about the lifecycles of personal and institutional aging. But it is also about discovering the wisdom to maintain youthful creative vitality no matter how chronologically old we and our institutions may be. Why a book on personal *and* institutional aging? Both journeys of aging are so inextricably and influentially intertwined that, in order to appreciate fully the challenges they separately and together face, they need to be jointly considered. The lifecycle experiences of personal aging provide invaluable insights into the ups and downs of institutional aging and vice versa.

In 1960 I met for the first time Cassie, my very elderly aunt, who lived in a remote village in Donegal, Ireland. As I came to know her better over a few weeks I became increasingly puzzled. In her long life she had suffered greatly from poverty, ill health, the deaths of family members whom she had cared for, and a multitude of changes in society. Humanly speaking, she had many reasons to be bitter in her old age. But she wasn't. Despite her advanced age, she maintained the youthfulness and vitality of a person seventy years younger. She remained interested in people of all ages. The beauty of the surrounding mauve-colored heather on the rolling, bog-pitted, and misty hillsides continued to surprise and delight her. And she seemed not to fear death.

Why, I thought, could someone of her age, infirmities, and background still be so youthful in outlook? Why, despite her limited education, had she become such a wise person? Finally, I asked her these two questions. She hesitated for a long time. Then she offered this short reply: "Read the scriptures. For decades I have listened to extracts from the Bible. One thing is sure for me: 'For God's foolishness is wiser than human wisdom.' Search the scriptures!" She smiled and said no more.

Now, fifty-three years later, in this book I seek to follow her advice. The scriptures do teach us how to remain youthful no matter how chronologically old we and our institutions may become.

The book has a second but related purpose, which I summarize in two questions: Why do cultures, organizations, even the church itself grow old and lose the vitality of youth? How can their youthfulness be restored? Anthropologist Claude Levi-Strauss's words about the dramatic decline of the New World's cities are relevant here: "They have one characteristic in common: that they pass from first youth to decrepitude with no intermediary stage."[1] This is so often the lot of institutions. They move with remarkable speed from youthful energy to signs of "decrepitude with no intermediary stage." Why does youthful energy disappear so fast? Why do we, as individuals and institutions, including the church, religious congregations, and ministries, pass so quickly from youthful energy to decrepitude? Why do some people, such as my late aunt Cassie, grow wiser and more youthful despite their ever-increasing physical infirmities? How can we, as individuals and institutions, acquire this wisdom? Why has the church, despite evidence of chaos, so quickly begun to experience again some tentative signs of youthfulness following the election of Pope Francis?

In attempting to answer these questions in light of the scriptures, I recalled that my aunt Cassie later said to me: "Gerald, the scriptures are all about loss and grief.[2] If we admit to loss, weep copiously, we can move on. That's the Irish way. That's the scriptural way."

Her comment reminded me of a common event in my boyhood. My family in the early days of World War II in

---

[1] Claude Levi-Strauss, *Tristes Tropiques: An Anthropological Study of Primitive Societies in Brazil*, trans. John Russell (New York: Atheneum, 1969), 100. I am grateful to Michael Jinkins for this insight. See his book *The Church Faces Death: Ecclesiology in a Post-Modern Context* (New York: Oxford University Press, 1999), 3.

[2] I have previously written on this theme in *Change, Grief, and Renewal in the Church: A Spirituality for a New Era* (Westminster: Christian Classics, 1991). However, this book significantly expands on the theme.

New Zealand lived close to a village where many Maori people had settled generations earlier. Very frequently I would be awakened by the ritual cries of women, wailing akin to the Irish keening. They were lamenting and mourning the deaths of loved ones. Their cries and copious tears would continue off and on for three days, but, following the funeral, there would be a huge feast and plenty of laughter. Former grievers would return to the world with their minds and hearts focused on the future. Like my aunt Cassie, these Maori people teach us the wisdom of mourning as a way to youthfulness, a wisdom that permeates every book of the scriptures.

From Loss to Youthfulness

There is no life without loss and therefore no life without grief.
—MIRIAM GREENSPAN,
HEALING THROUGH THE DARK EMOTIONS

Most changes, even if people intellectually assent to them, necessitate loss or bereavement, and loss evokes grief. A clear distinction, however, must be made between *grieving* and *mourning. Grieving* or *grief* describes the internal emotions of sadness, sorrow, anger, anguish, confusion, shame, even guilt that results from our experiences of loss.[3] Grief is pain. It is loneliness, emptiness. It is fear. Many kinds of loss can occur one on top of the other, such as poor health, loss of work, death of loved ones, breakdown of relationships, the loss of self-worth, the inability to defend oneself

---

[3] The words *grief* and *grieving* have the same meaning in this book, unless otherwise qualified.

against the onslaughts of bullying in its many faces, so grief can accumulate and become overwhelming. Grief is thus not confined to death experiences, though many griefs presage the definitive loss through death. Every time we grieve, we are asked to let go of some familiar and cherished part of ourselves, and this can be hard. But grief is a normal part of life, a necessary consequence of being alive. Grief is not a sickness any more than joy is.

Mourning, on the other hand, shows us how we are to handle grief positively. It embraces two simultaneous and complementary dynamics. First, it refers to the culturally patterned external expressions or rituals that publicly acknowledge that loss and grief have occurred to the bereaved.[4] Second, it connotes the agonizing inner journey that the bereaved must make to let go of their attachment to what is lost in order to be able to move on in life. Loss evokes contradictory impulses with which the process of mourning must grapple.

On the one hand, there is the urge to cling tenaciously to what is lost and to that which gave meaning to one's life, even to deny that loss has occurred. On the other hand, there is the need to rebuild a way of life or new relationships in which what was positive from the past is maintained and even revitalized. The word *mourning,* therefore, as distinct from *grieving,* refers to what people do to manage their grief externally through rituals and internally through transforming their relationships with what has been lost. Depending on the depth of the loss, these processes may take significant time and conscious effort.

---

[4] See Kenneth J. Doka and Terry L. Martin, *Grieving Beyond Gender: Understanding the Ways Men and Women Mourn* (New York: Routledge, 2010), 28–30.

Not just individuals but also cultures of all kinds experience grief as they grow old. Unless this grief can be publicly articulated in mourning rituals it will haunt the living, lead to all kinds of de-energizing and dysfunctional behavior, and destroy every spirit of youthfulness. The unvoiced grief of individuals and cultures has insidious consequences, evoking untold heartache and anxiety.[5] It is of overriding significance for people to be able to express this pain freely and unashamedly before people who understand.[6] This is a central theme of this book.

An example illustrates this point. One day in 1987 I visited the central square of Onset, a small village in Massachusetts, where an anonymous veteran had erected a large notice board on which had been painted these words:

> Please understand that we are not asking for a parade, a monument or pity. But we do ask you to remember in your own way the 58,129 Americans who died in the [Vietnam] war. . . . We as individuals and as a nation learned something of human value for having been in SE Asia. Give us space to mourn.

Trapped in a political struggle that should have been decided before they risked their lives, soldiers returning from Vietnam often felt in shock a second time when they were confronted by public rejection of the war in which they had fought and seen their colleagues wounded and killed. All they were asking for was the public space to tell their stories. Without this, there could be no final healing.

---

[5] See ibid., 18–25. See also Therese A. Rando, *Treatment of Complicated Mourning* (Champaign, IL: Research Press, 1993), 146–47, 177–78, 185–240, 380–81, 584.

[6] See C. Charles Bachmann, *Ministering to the Grief Sufferer* (Philadelphia: Fortress Press, 1964), 46–51.

They could not openly mourn and move forward as long as the government refused to admit it had morally and militarily lost the war. The government had repeatedly refused to build a memorial to those killed in the Vietnam war because to do so would mean acknowledging that the nation had failed.[7] Hence, critically important lessons for the nation's future remained unlearned, and thousands of veterans and their families had to grieve privately, their inner pain and the truth about the nation's guilt ignored.

If mourning rituals are not publicly permitted, then the heartrending inner pilgrimage of letting go of undue attachments to the past cannot take place. The bereaved—whether individuals, organizations, cultures, or nations—will remain emotionally trapped in the past. As sociologist Peter Marris, a specialist in loss and mourning, writes: "The management of change depends upon our ability to articulate the process of grieving [in mourning rituals]. . . . When loss cannot be articulated, its suppressed tensions will in the end prove more profoundly disruptive than the social conflicts which relieve them"[8] As the wise Roman poet Ovid (43 BCE–17 CE) wrote centuries ago: "Suppressed grief suffocates."[9] When grieving over loss cannot be expressed through mourning rituals, "there is a corresponding disappearance of passion for life and of the strength and intensity of its joys" and intuitions.[10] Tennyson articulates simply this crucial advice: "Ring out the grief that saps the mind."[11] And in the words of the psalmist:

---

[7] A memorial was eventually constructed in Washington DC, but by private initiative and financing.

[8] Peter Marris, *Loss and Change* (London: Routledge and Kegan Paul, 1974), 91, 103.

[9] Ovid, *Tristia*, Book V, eleg. 1, ln. 63.

[10] Dorothee Soelle, *Suffering* (Philadelphia: Fortress Press, 1975), 36.

[11] Alfred Tennyson, *In Memoriam*, cvi.st.3.

> Weeping may linger for the night,
>   but joy comes with the morning. . . .
> You have turned my mourning into dancing.
>   (Ps 30:5, 11)

Through mourning we can rediscover inner peace, joy, and the energy to move forward in hope to a revitalized youthful spirit. True, we must not forget the past and its lessons. But we must be released from excessive attachment to it.

Application to the People of God

We as the people of God have been experiencing for decades an overload of accumulated and unarticulated grief. Our efforts to process this grief through mourning rituals have too often been forbidden by hierarchical officials who have wished to maintain order at all costs. Yet denial and suppression of grief have only intensified the sadness and rage in our hearts. Youthful energy for the mission of Christ has been suffocated.

Ponder what has been happening. Within and outside the church over the last sixty years we have experienced change after change, loss after loss. We grieve over the fact that the self-confident euphoria for the reform of the church following Vatican II all but evaporated until the coming of Pope Francis. We grieve over the widespread loss of interest in the message of Christ. For secularists, our churches are quaint reminders of a world that is gone; in the eyes of many, we are useful for providing charity for people who are poor, nothing else. As attendance at religious services dramatically declines, we grieve over the closure of once thriving parish churches where for generations our families have worshiped. We grieve over the fact that we have contributed to the alienation of peoples from Christ through our reluctance, as individuals and faith communities, to cooperate with the Holy Spirit in calling for innovative pastoral action. We grieve the exclusive emphases and often unintelligible changes in our liturgies. We grieve over lost opportunities to preach Christ's message of love and justice.

Although the Eucharist is the heart of our faith communities, we grieve that countless communities are without priests. We grieve the rapid diminishment of once flourishing religious congregations. We grieve because women have yet to have their rightful place in ministries. We grieve the loss of credibility and trust in the church resulting from the frequently published scandals of sexual abuse of youth and the failures of hierarchies to respond with justice and charity to this horrible evil; from the administrative bullying abuses of the Roman Curia; and from the refusal by hierarchical officials to allow public expressions of mourning for these losses. While we applaud the commitment of Pope Francis to reform the curia, we grieve the failure of many dioceses to act collegially. We can become so overwhelmed by these losses that our hearts become numbed and our energies drained by the struggle to restore that which has been irretrievably lost.

What can we do as the people of God—as individuals, institutions and ministries—to overcome efforts to deny and suppress this grief? When it comes to acknowledging the sadness of loss, most of us stutter meaningless comments like "I don't know what to say." We yearn to ring out the griefs that are sapping our energies for mission, but we do not know how. We are "greatly disturbed in spirit and deeply moved" (John 11:33), as Jesus was at the sight of Mary weeping over the death of her brother, Lazarus, but we do not know how to mourn openly like Jesus because we have so often been officially forbidden to do so. Yet the scriptures have a simple, but profound, even paradoxical, answer. We are invited to mourn our losses through complaining! Did not Jesus on the cross agonizingly and so publicly complain to the Father in the words of Psalm 22: "My God, my God, why have you forsaken me?" (Matt 27:46).

The lament psalms teach us how to complain in the midst of the dark nights of our overwhelming sadness. Our loud, faith-based complaints become in themselves rituals of mourning through which our griefs are abandoned and we can to the future again in hope. Not to complain, as the scriptures teach us, means that we will continue to be haunted, suffocated, by our sorrows. We will be destroyed, overwhelmed, by the unarticulated pain of our powerlessness. Yet, if we truly complain to God from the very depths and emptiness of our souls, trusting in God's willingness to listen, hope will come alive once more. Ponder the public lament of the Israelites as they agonizingly view the destruction of the pivotal symbol of God's presence, the Temple. Desolation reigns supreme. God gets all the blame, but once their sadness has been so dramatically proclaimed and put aside, the Israelites discover space within their hearts for a hopeful trust in God:

> O God, why do you cast us off forever?
>> Why does your anger smoke against
>> the sheep of your pasture? . . .
> Your foes have roared within your holy
>> place; . . .
> And then, with hatchets and hammers,
>> they smashed all its carved work. . . .
> Rise up, O God, plead your cause;
> remember how the impious scoff at you all
>> the day long. (Ps 74:1, 4, 6, 22)

To lament demands that we put aside our denials of loss, but this is difficult in our loss-repudiating Western cultures, including at times in our liturgies, which often avoid the challenging, often harsh but paradoxically hope-filled language of lament. Walter Brueggemann comments: "Such a denial and cover-up . . . is an odd inclination for passionate Bible users, given the large number of psalms that are songs of lament, protest, and complaint about the incoherence that is experienced in the world. At least it is clear that a church that goes on singing 'happy songs' in the face of raw reality is doing something very different from what the Bible itself does."[12]

We need to look very closely at the cultures to which we belong, including our church cultures, because we can be negatively and unconsciously influenced by the ways they deny or avoid the realities of loss. This is why people in traditional cultures, such as those we find in Africa, Asia, and the South Pacific, have so much to reteach us about how to relate to significant losses. For these cultures loss is something that affects not just individuals but the groups to which they belong; failure to mourn the dual impact is to be haunted by the past. Mourning is a duty that people must publicly undertake.

Influenced and infused with hope by Pope Francis, this book is about aging and how to rekindle biblical youthfulness within the people of God. When Vatican II proclaimed that the church is the people of God, it focused on the communal family nature of the church, that is, God relating to people, no matter what their position in the church, rather than focusing exclusively on the church's hierarchical and institutional aspects. In fact, "the hierarchical structure of

---

[12] Walter Brueggemann, *The Message of the Psalms* (Minneapolis: Augsburg, 1984), 51–52.

the Church exists to serve the whole people of God, not to dominate or control it."[13] Through baptism, people who believe are reborn as a fresh community, God's chosen ones,[14] and this people of God participates in Christ's offices of priest, prophet, and servant-king (*LG*, nos. 10–12). All humankind is invited to be part of this people of God (*LG*, no. 13). Though the emphasis in the council was on the Roman Catholic Church, it also acknowledges that God's grace is present in other churches and ecclesial communities (*LG*, no. 15). Consequently, this book is about the aging of this family of God—its individual members and its multitude of its institutions—and the ways in which all family members can rediscover the revitalizing power of wisdom through lament.

Scriptural Wisdom: "The Francis Factor"

> *Therefore teach me wisdom in my secret heart.*
>
> —PSALM 51:6

Philosophically, wisdom is "the fruit of patient reflection on experience. It is insight into the order of nature and history so well-developed that it can be the rule of life."[15] Thus wisdom is something more than raw information or

---

[13] Richard P. McBrien, *The Church: The Evolution of Catholicism* (New York: HarperOne, 2008), 167.

[14] Vatican II, *Dogmatic Constitution on the Church* (*Lumen Gentium*), ed. Austin P. Flannery, *Documents of Vatican II* (Grand Rapids, MI: Eerdmans, 1975), no. 9. Quotations from Vatican II documents are from this source.

[15] Eugen Biser, "Wisdom," in *Encyclopedia of Theology: A Concise Sacramentum Mundi*, ed. Karl Rahner (London: Burns and Oates, 1975), 1818.

understanding. As Plato says in the *Phaedo*, "Wisdom is the harmony of intellect and will based on self-knowledge." Wisdom is information and understanding gained through *contemplation* on experience that will guide behavior. It is a form of understanding that combines a reflective attitude and a practical concern to act virtuously.

While wisdom can and must draw on the insights of human reason, ultimately true wisdom comes from the contemplation of God's revelation in Christ Jesus. This is the import of Saint Paul's advice to which my aunt Cassie referred:

> For God's foolishness is wiser than human wisdom, and God's weakness is stronger than human strength. Consider your own call brothers and sisters: not many of you were wise by human standards. . . . But God chose what is foolish in the world to shame the wise. (1 Cor 1:25, 27)

This is the wisdom that my aunt Cassie stored in her heart. It is the wisdom that will guide the reflections on aging in this book. It is also the wisdom about which Pope Francis speaks . . . and lives by.

The Structure of This Book

The book is intended to assist a wide range of people in their various ministries, such as bishops, theologians, liturgists, applied anthropologists, pastoral workers, and staff members in schools, healthcare, business organizations, and tertiary institutions.

The book draws on several disciplines, including theology, scripture, history, and, particularly, cultural anthropology.

I provide examples throughout the text from traditional and Western societies to illustrate the theory I am proposing, so the book will be of pastoral assistance for people in many cultures. Anthropology is about how people feel and communicate with one another and across cultures. It is often about revealing the cultural forces that motivate people and their institutions, although they are commonly unaware of the existence of these forces and their ability to affect behavior.[16] Cultural anthropology has been called by anthropologist Raymond Firth "an inquisitive, challenging, uncomfortable discipline, questioning established positions . . . peering into underlying interests, if not destroying fictions and empty phrases . . . at least exposing them."[17] I hope readers find that the following pages testify to the accuracy of this description.

There are seven chapters, five of which conclude with a theological reflection. Chapter 1, "Scriptural Wisdom: From Aging to Youthfulness," points out that in the scriptures, especially in the Old Testament, aging is a quality not only of individuals but also of collective groups of people and institutions. The scriptures are filled with incidents describing symptoms of aging and the myriad, depressing losses that so often accompany it. At the same time there is inspiring and sage advice about how to deal with these symptoms.

The next chapter, "Aging in Cultures: The Universal Call to Let Go" has two aims: (1) to review sociologically and briefly the different approaches in Western and traditional cultures to aging; and (2) to summarize the wisdom of Saint Teresa on aging—the ways to let go of those attachments

---

[16] See Gerald A. Arbuckle, *Culture, Inculturation, and Theologians: A Postmodern Critique* (Collegeville, MN: Liturgical Press, 2010), 19–48.

[17] Raymond Firth, "Engagement and Detachment: Reflections on Applying Social Anthropology to Social Affairs," *Human Organization* 40 (1981): 200.

that hinder or stop people and institutions, at any age, from receiving God-given youthfulness.

The third chapter, "Faces of Grief: Grief's Suffocating Power" explains why *grief* is a difficult word to describe; it is something felt and so cannot be satisfactorily confined to a neat definition. Indeed, grief has many expressions, and if unarticulated, people and institutions become paralyzed. When this happens to institutions, we speak of cultural trauma or collective depression. But although with the death of Jesus the small group of disciples hid in fear, Jesus had left the message that in hope they could break through the trauma.

"Grappling with Loss: From Grieving to New Life," Chapter 4, describes the three tasks in a fruitful mourning process: the struggle of the bereaved to let go what has been lost; the redefining of the bereaved identity in view of the loss; and behavioral consequences of the redefining. Mourning rituals are shaped according to public values of particular cultures. Traditional cultures have much to teach Western societies in how to mourn positively. The lament psalms provide a template for mourning for believers; they are prayers in which the psalmist grapples with personal loss or cultural trauma, deciding whether to cling to what has been lost or to let go and be open in trust to the newness that God is offering.

The following chapter, "Aging Institutions: Can Youthfulness Return?" offers a model of what happens to an institution when grieving losses are not permitted; suppressed grief ends in cultural trauma. But the impasse created by cultural trauma can be broken by the right leadership. The spirituality of Saint John of the Cross shows us how to relate constructively to this impasse.

Chapter 6, "The 'Francis Factor': Re-owning the Vatican II Story," applies the model of suppressed grief and cultural trauma to the Catholic Church since Vatican II. The Roman Curia was primarily responsible for embedding our conciliar mythology, but as the curia remained unreformed, the residual pre-conciliar mythology increasingly resurfaced. Public mourning through responsible dissent was forbidden. Pope Francis, by his actions and words, is breaking through the impasse, allowing the people of God to mourn openly and to hope for newness based on the mythology of Vatican II. The theological reflection that concludes this chapter draws on the wisdom of Saint Ignatius Loyola.

The final chapter, "From Mourning to Joy: The Ministry of Leadership," focuses on the importance of scriptural foundations for mourning rituals and offers practical pastoral advice for leaders about how these rituals can be shaped for parishes and other ministries.

1

Scriptural Wisdom

From Aging to Youthfulness

*You desire truth in the inward being;
therefore teach me wisdom in my secret
 heart.*

—PSALM 51:6

*Beginning with Abraham . . . the divine
call turns human beings into sojourn-
ers, in pilgrims on a journey into the
unknown, guided only by trust in an
often elusive God. . . . In consenting
to the call . . . believers do not give up
their freedom; they acquire it to the
full.*

—JOHN OF TAIZE, *A NEW TESTAMENT*

Key points covered in this chapter

- Aging in the scriptures is a journey of letting go undue
  attachments that hold us back from knowing and serving God; this is true wisdom, a gift that ultimately comes
  from God. In order to let go these attachments, we must
  develop the art of mourning in faith and hope.

- The Old Testament describes in vivid language the physical and emotional challenges of aging.
- Both Testaments insist that we are obliged to care for aging people.
- In the New Testament wisdom is Christ himself; through his life, death, and resurrection we learn the art of authentic mourning into youthfulness.

In the scriptures, especially in the Old Testament, aging is a quality not only of individuals but also of collective groups of people and institutions. They all have one thing in common: all are on a journey. Ever since the time when Abram was called by God to leave his country and go to the land that would be shown him (Gen 12:1), the scriptures are filled with incidents describing the symptoms of aging and the myriad, depressing losses that so often accompany it. There are references to the ultimate consequences of the journey of aging, that is, death, either the physical death of a person or metaphorical death, such as personal and national estrangement from God through sin, sickness, plagues, famine, wars, or exile.

At the same time there is sage advice about how to deal well with these symptoms of aging. Let go of attachments to idols of power, wealth, and embrace God's will. This is the gift of mourning: "Put on sackcloth, and roll in ashes; make mourning . . . most bitter lamentation" (Jer 6:26). Then God "will turn . . . mourning into joy" (Jer 32:13). The inner liveliness of youthfulness will return, though paradoxically the physical signs may remain and even intensify. To refuse this call to mourn is to rebuff God's wisdom: "We wailed," cries Jesus, "and you did not weep" (Luke 7:31). For those who embrace this invitation there is this reply: "Blessed are those who mourn, for they shall be comforted" (Matt 5:4).

Collective Aging

The Israelite creation myth is this: God has a special love for the chosen people and their institutions. The Israelites must respond to this love, especially through worship and justice to people who are poor and marginalized. They are the people of God: "You only have I known of all the families of the earth" (Amos 3:2). When the Israelites collectively forget this message, they are overwhelmed by terrifying darkness or chaos. The period in the wilderness after the joyful departure from Egypt is the archetypal experience of the chaos that can periodically destroy their original youthful exuberance, leaving them with the bitterness and loss of energy often associated with old age (Exod 16—18): travelers without a sense of direction, bickering with one another, directing anger at God and their leaders, hungry, prey to all kinds of diseases and attacks from outsiders, feeling the sense of rootlessness. They yearn for land to call their own and the chance to grow their own good-tasting food. In such misery even the oppression of Egypt seems heavenly, as they complain to Moses: "If only we had died by the hand of the Lord in the land of Egypt, when we sat by the fleshpots and ate our fill of bread; for you have brought us out into this wilderness to kill this whole assembly with hunger" (Exod 16:3). Once they mourn their sinfulness, their attachments to false gods, they are then able to acknowledge their dependence on a loving and compassionate God. Then their youthful vitality returns.

The exile into Babylon is the next horrible experience of chaos. With the destruction of the three pivotal institutional symbols of their faith, thought to be eternal witnesses to God's abiding presence and promise of lasting youth—the kingship, the Temple, and Jerusalem—the people move into depression, anger, sadness, guilt, scapegoating, numbness, and pain beyond description: "By the rivers of Babylon—there we sat down and there we wept when we remembered Zion. . . . How could we sing the Lord's song in a foreign land?" (Ps 137:1, 4). They nostalgically dream of their earlier years of youthful, energizing joy without worries, the feeling that life would continue without interruption under God's abiding care. One can almost hear the Israelites sitting together, exhausted after slaving all day under the relentless and tyrannical bullying of their foreign masters and weighed down with guilt, self-reproach and shame, wistfully and nostalgically recounting stories of the great days of their youth in their own land.

Weariness and Rest

Walter Brueggemann helpfully explains that for the Israelites the experience of chaos, the antithesis of rest, is often described as weariness. They are weary when they want to live an *ordered* life that takes no account of God's plans for them. They lack the wisdom that comes from pondering and following God's will in their lives: "Truly, with stammering lip and with alien tongue he will speak to this people, to whom he has said, 'This is rest: give rest to the weary; and this is repose'; yet they would not hear" (Isa 28:11–12). They stay stubbornly foolish, condemned to remain weary: "Hear this, O foolish and senseless people, who have eyes, but do not see, who have ears, but do not hear" (Jer 5:21). In Lamentations weariness is the feeling of being the slave to a false master, while rest connotes wisdom and service to the one true God: "With a yoke on our necks we are hard driven; we are weary, we are given no rest" (Lam 5:5). After examining many texts, Brueggemann comments that "it is clear that *weariness* refers to a time of misery and trouble of drastic proportions and *rest* means a context of security and well-being." The texts show that only God's powerful intervention or that of God's agent can remove the state of chaotic despairing weariness and revitalize their youthfulness: "These texts play upon an old mythological pattern of chaos and creation."[1]

Wisdom in Chaos

Throughout the scriptures God is pictured as actually allowing chaos to develop as the preface or catalyst for a marked creative faith response and growth in wisdom. In the darkness of chaos the people have the chance once more to encounter God, the founder of the nation and the source of energizing hope, and discard what is not essential to their founding story. No matter how decrepit they may have become as a nation, they are able to rediscover in the confusion that the following of God's will is the unique source of authentic wisdom.

In the national disarray they are forced to reexperience that they are emotionally, physically, and spiritually fragile, and that God alone is the ultimate source of youthful vitality. Struggling under the scorching sun "in a land of deserts and pits, in a land of drought and deep darkness" (Jer 2:6), "an arid wasteland with poisonous snakes and scorpions" (Deut 8:15), the Israelites are challenged to face their foolishness and loss of wisdom: "As for mortals, their days are like grass; they flourish like a flower of the field; for the

---

[1] Walter Brueggemann, "Weariness, Exile, and Chaos: A Motif in Royal Theology," *The Catholic Biblical Quarterly* 34 (1972): 72; see also idem, "Kingship and Chaos: A Study in Tenth Century Theology," *The Catholic Biblical Quarterly* 33 (1971): 317–32.

wind passes over it, and it is gone, and its place knows it no more" (Ps 103:15–16). In the language of Deuteronomy: "He humbled you by letting you hunger, then by feeding you with manna, with which neither you nor your ancestors were acquainted, in order to make you understand that one does not live by bread alone, but by every word that comes from the mouth of the Lord" (Deut 8:3).

Jeremiah is referred to as the prophet of chaos; he looked on the nation around him "and lo, it was waste and void" (Jer 4:23). Not only is Israel socially and politically corrupted from within through cheating and oppression, but it is threatened by invasion from outside.[2] Yet, at the same time, Jeremiah foresees new life if only the people would collectively return to their covenant partner—God: "See, today I appoint you over nations and over kingdoms . . . to overthrow, to build and to plant" (Jer 1:10). If the Israelites grasp and re-own this truth of God's abiding love for them, they will again possess the true wisdom of God's people.

Personal Aging and Community Support

> *Remember your creator in the days of your youth, before the days of trouble come, and the years draw near when you will say, "I have no pleasure in them"; . . . strong men are bent; . . . and those who look through the windows see dimly; . . . when one is afraid of heights, and terrors are in the road . . .*

---

[2] See Robert P. Carroll, *From Chaos to Covenant: Prophecy in the Book of Jeremiah* (New York: Crossroad, 1981), 66.

and dust returns to the earth . . . and
the breath returns to God who gave it.
—ECCLESIASTES 12:1, 3, 5, 7

From time to time in the Old Testament individuals are graphically described with the physical frailties that are usually associated with chronological aging: gray hair, weakening eyesight and hearing, loss of physical strength and taste, the demise of sexual powers.[3]

- Samuel says: "I am old and gray" (1 Sam 12:2).
- As they aged, Isaac and Israel both lost the ability to see. When Isaac became old "his eyes were dim so that he could not see" (Gen 27:1); of Israel, we read that his eyes "were dim with age, and he could not see well" (Gen 48:10).
- Sarah mockingly laughs: "After I have grown old, and my husband is old, shall I have pleasure?" (Gen 18:12).
- Moses, however, was singularly untouched by the process of aging: "Moses was one hundred twenty years old when he died; his sight was unimpaired and his vigor had not abated" (Deut 34:7).

Then there are the psychological weaknesses of aging, such as the loss of independence, or the fears of burdening others with their care. Barzillai, a faithful defender of David, hesitates to accept David's hospitality because of his aging. He complains that he is no longer mentally alert and feels he is a burden to others: "Today I am eighty years old; can I discern what is pleasant and what is not? Can your servant

---

[3] In this chapter I am deeply indebted to Rachel Z. Dulin for her excellent analysis on aging in the Old Testament. See *A Crown of Glory: A Biblical View of Aging* (New York: Paulist Press, 1988).

taste what he eats or what he drinks? Can I listen to the voice of singing men and women? Why should your servant be an added burden to my lord the king?" (2 Sam 19:35). Even the great Solomon declined mentally and began to act imprudently, all because of his aging (1 Kings 11:4–10).

The traditional Hebrew family, like most pre-modern family systems (see Chapter 2), was patriarchal and extended well beyond the nuclear unit of parents and children to include the clan and tribe. It was impossible to imagine life and personal identity outside this extended family system.[4] In fact, the individual depended completely on the family for identity, support, and protection. Roles within the family system were socially predetermined and interdependent, so that even the elderly had definite and prominent responsibilities.[5] In theory grandparents and parents filled the key role of passing on the tribal and family wisdom, but this did not always happen, so people had to be reminded of their obligations. In particular, members of the younger generation had to be reminded often of their serious duties to *both* parents: "Honor your father and your mother, so that your days may be long in the land" (Exod 20:12). Likewise, in Proverbs: "Listen to your father who begot you, and do not despise your mother when she is old" (Prov 23:22). Failure to honor parents could lead to banishment, loss of identity, poverty, and even death (Deut 21:18–21).[6]

This is why in the scriptures, including the New Testament, there are quite detailed rules regarding inheritance

---

[4] See Gerald A. Arbuckle, *Earthing the Gospel: An Inculturation Handbook for Pastoral Workers* (Maryknoll, NY: Orbis Books, 1990), 46–47.

[5] See Dulin, *A Crown of Glory,* 54–69.

[6] In Isaiah, God severely reprimands the Babylonians for not caring for the elderly Israelites: "I gave them into your hand, you showed them no mercy; on the aged you made your yoke exceedingly heavy" (47:6).

and disinheritance.[7] Inheritance must not be used by individuals at the expense of the needs of kinsfolk.[8] The emphasis on mutuality of roles explicitly means that care must be extended to aging family members. The honor of the family demanded this; to do otherwise would be considered most shameful for all concerned.[9] The crucial importance of caring for the elderly is evident in the prophet Isaiah's foretelling of the downfall of the Babylonian Empire; it would self-destruct precisely because it oppressed the elderly, which in the estimate of the Israelites was most evil: "I gave them into your hand, you showed them no mercy; on the aged you made your yoke exceedingly heavy" (Isa 47:6). In Deuteronomy the author had foretold this terrible thing would happen: "The Lord will bring a nation from far away . . . to swoop down on you . . . showing no respect to the old or favor to the young" (Deut 28:49–50).

The Call to Pray!

In short, for the Old Testament writers, personal aging is a time of inescapable ailments and emotional turmoil. This

---

[7] See Jonathan Burnside, *God, Justice, and Society: Aspects of Law and Legality in the Bible* (Oxford: Oxford University Press, 2011), 183, 190–92. The parable of the prodigal son in the New Testament is an example of a bitter domestic quarrel about inheritance and its correct use. See Gerald A. Arbuckle, *Laughing with God: Humor, Culture, and Transformation* (Collegeville, MN: Liturgical Press, 2004), 78–80.

[8] In the parable of the rich fool, the stupidity of the greedy farmer who wants to hoard his grain only for his own benefit, ignoring the needs of his extended family, is condemned by Jesus (Luke 12:13–20).

[9] See Jerome H. Neyrey, "Loss of Wealth, Loss of Family, Loss of Honor: The Cultural Context of the Original Makarisms in Q," in *The Social World of the New Testament,* ed. Jerome H. Neyrey and Eric C. Stewart (Peabody, MA: Hendrickson Publishers, 2008), 87–102.

is well described in two heartrending psalms (71 and 90) that specifically focus on the challenges of aging. Psalm 71 emphasizes the social implications of aging and the irritations that the elderly feel as they experience the increasing weaknesses of aging. The author of Psalm 90 philosophically ponders the frustration he feels because of the brevity of time between birth and death.

Despite the many sadnesses and fears of becoming old, both psalms end with an expression of hope because they trust God's loving providence. Both are lament psalms;[10] that is, they arise out of the depths of human experience: suffering, pain, despair, and torment. God is suddenly absent, but Israelites privately and publicly complain this should no longer be the situation. God *must* act to help the chosen people, as was the case in the times of the Exodus. God initiated a relationship, and the Israelites at prayer seek to hold God to this agreement. God is a friend, and with friends there is no need to camouflage or conceal reality. God must hear the turmoil of aging in all its anguish, because as a true friend God will understand. Hence, the language of lament psalms is robust and audaciously bold. For example, Psalm 13 begins: "How long, O Lord? Will you forget me forever? . . . How long must I bear pain in my soul . . . all day long?" (13:1–2).

Psalm 71: Grief: Loneliness and Weaknesses of the Elderly

In the Old Testament aging "is in itself a kind of grief, bringing home in graphic lines . . . the fact that as the past increases, the future decreases. As the years take their toll, the things that were once easy may become more difficult

---

[10] The nature of lament or complaining psalms will be more fully explained in Chapter 4.

or even impossible."[11] This is poignantly evident in lament Psalm 71.[12] The author as an old man begs for defense against enemies who are hounding him: "O Lord, do not delay!" (v. 1). He poignantly prays: "Do not cast me off in the time of old age; do not forsake me when my strength is spent" (v. 9). As an old man he recognizes that society is no longer interested in his protection because he is physically weakened and without power: "They say, 'Pursue and seize that person whom God has forsaken, for there is no one to deliver'" (v. 11). Now in his old age he feels lonely and defenseless, socially cast aside because he no longer has the vigor and power of youth. What particularly concerns the writer is not so much his escape from those who want to kill him, but rather the fear that God may desert him now that he is old: "So even to old age and gray hairs, O God, do not forsake me, until I proclaim your might to all generations to come" (v. 18).

The psalmist is shrewdly aware that as an old person he has the wisdom that physically strong and younger people lack. The older people become, the more they can speak from experience of God's ongoing faithfulness and righteousness: "All day long my tongue will talk of your righteous help, for those who tried to do me harm have been put to shame, and disgraced" (v. 24). God is a righteous God because the psalmist knows from experience something that the young have yet to learn: God is one who intervenes to restore well-being.[13] The psalmist's lifelong experience of

---

[11] Merren Parker, *A Time to Grieve* (Auckland: Methuen, 1981), 20.

[12] This psalm, along with most lament psalms, is classed as an individual psalm; that is, it is a cry to God from an individual in distress. Most individual laments conclude with the belief that God has heard the prayer.

[13] See Walter Brueggemann, *Reverberations of Faith: A Theological Handbook of Old Testament Themes* (Louisville, KY: Westminster John Knox Press, 2002), 179.

God's saving righteousness gives him hope that his enemies will eventually be put to shame. The psalmist, through God's intervention, will be able to fulfill an elder's duty, namely, the task of ensuring that coming generations know of God's ever-faithful righteousness to those who act justly.

In summary, the psalmist complains that in his old age he is the prey of the vindictive and unjust. He begs God to watch over him in his increasing infirmities; just as God protected him when he was young, he asks that God do the same now that he is weak. He is confident that God will rescue him from those who wish to harm him. He trusts in God's protecting hand: "Be to me a rock of refugee, a strong fortress, to save me, for you are my rock and my fortress" (v. 3). Thus, although the psalmist is terribly conscious of his physical and emotional aging, the very fact that he can articulate his fears and emotional turmoil makes him feel once again internally youthful.

Psalm 90: Community and Personal Transience, Sin, and Wisdom

This psalm is both a communal[14] and personal prayer. The community and individual Israelites, conscious of their sinfulness and affliction, are in desperate need of God's help, for they have been in turmoil for a long time with no humanly known way to move forward. They are at an impasse: "Turn, O Lord! How long? Have compassion on your servants! . . . Make us glad as many days as you have afflicted us, and as many years as we have seen evil" (Ps 90:13, 15). The nation and all Israelites must face the judgment of

---

[14] Psalm 90 is classed as a community prayer; that is, it is a prayer that the community would recite in times of great national catastrophe, for example, a harvest failure, a military emergency, or a plague.

an all-seeing God because of their sinfulness: "For we are consumed by your anger; by you wrath we are overwhelmed. You have set our iniquities before you, our secret sins in the light of your countenance" (vv. 7–8).

However, they are conscious that time is not on their side. They repent and mourn their failures: "For all our days pass away under your wrath; our years come to an end like a sigh. The days of our life are seventy years or perhaps eighty, if we are strong" (vv. 9–10). Life is so short; it is "like grass . . . in the morning it flourishes and is renewed; in the evening it fades and withers" (v. 6–7). Then, before it is too late comes the frantic prayer for wisdom: "So teach us to count our days that we may gain a wise heart" (v. 12). A wise heart refers to the gift of discernment whereby people are able to discover and follow God's will in their lives. In order to balance the community's distress and despair, and motivated by this wisdom, the people trust God, whose all-powerful presence is "from everlasting to everlasting" (v. 2). God is trusted because the Israelites are not homeless and lonely since God is actually their shelter or home: "Lord, you have been our dwelling place in all generations" (v. 1).[15] Brueggemann, when commenting on the words "wise heart," says that wisdom means that God *is* our home, not just an awareness of our human fragility and guilt.[16] Since God *is* home, home existed before the world was created: "Before the mountains were brought forth, or ever you had formed the earth and the world, from everlasting to everlasting you are God" (v. 2). For the poet, this is an awesome and humbling truth! Who are we in comparison with the eternal power of God, who was God before even the world

---

[15] See Walter Brueggemann, *The Message of the Psalms: A Theological Commentary* (Minneapolis: Augsburg, 1984), 111.

[16] Ibid., 112.

was formed and who will continue to be God when it has ceased to exist?

Despite the "many years as we have seen evil" (v. 15), the breathtaking creative power of God will again "be manifest to his servants (v. 16); God will still "prosper for us the work of our hands!" (v. 17).[17] The psalmist is no longer seeking political supremacy for the nation but only "the simple happiness of being allowed to enjoy in peace the work of their hands; undisturbed, that is, by greedy tax-collectors and moneylenders and armies on the march."[18] The peace that the psalmist pleads for is not synonymous with passivity, to retire in one's declining years to do nothing. On the contrary, since this is a lament psalm the psalmist is insistent that fidelity to God's will is the relentless struggle to do good and seek justice.[19] Lament does not mean resignation to the status quo.

This is an astonishingly energizing prayer for people at all times and centuries who are suddenly conscious of their aging. They yearn in the short time remaining to them to contemplate God's loving patience and accomplish good deeds. They no longer crave to dominate those around them; they are not motivated by greed and material well-being. This is their hope. It is our hope today! It is a psalm that calls us to love tenderly and work for justice no matter how elderly we may be: "He has told you, O mortal, what is good: . . . to do justice, and to love kindness, and to walk humbly with your God" (Mic 6:8). It is not a call, no matter what our age and infirmities may be, to retire complacently from desiring and doing good in the name of God.

---

[17] See Bernhard W. Anderson, *Out of the Depths: The Psalms Speak for Us Today* (Philadelphia: Westminster Press, 1983), 228–30.

[18] Sigmund Mowinckel, *The Psalms in Israel's Worship*, trans. D. R. Ap-Thomas (Oxford: Basil Blackwell, 1982), 102.

[19] See Brueggemann, *The Message of the Psalms*, 115.

In summary, the psalmist complains that life is too fleeting: "Our years come to an end like a sigh. The days of our life are seventy years, or perhaps eighty, if we are strong" (Ps 90:9, 10). Even the time we have is overwhelmed by toil and worry. The psalmist begs God to save him from annihilation before his appointed time has been reached, but he is confident that, no matter what happens, his descendants will be safe and give God the praise that he finds so difficult to articulate in the midst of his present suffering and old age.

Old Age and Wisdom

> *Vanity of vanities, says the Teacher; all is vanity. . . . The sayings of the wise are like goads. . . . Fear God, and keep his commandments.*
> —ECCLESIASTES 12:8, 11, 13

In the Old Testament old age is described as a blessing, a gift of life that reaches fullness despite the fact that the period is marked by so many disabilities. As explained above, the psalmist begs God for the blessing of wisdom as his journey in life progresses inexorably to its conclusion (Ps 90:12). The wisdom that the psalmist yearns for has a prophetic quality, namely, the ability to see the world as God sees it. This means rejecting the values of a corrupt society, a society that refuses to follow the commandments of God.[20] God promises this wisdom to those who are faithful: "Even to your old age I am he, even when you turn gray I will carry you. . . . I will carry and will save" (Isa

---

[20] See Marcus J. Borg, *Meeting Jesus Again for the First Time* (New York: HarperOne, 1994), 98–102.

46:4). Wisdom, therefore, is supposed to be a quality of the elderly, but in the scriptures it is by no means an automatic gift of aging. It can even be lost in old age, as we see in the story of Solomon whose original "wisdom surpassed the wisdom of all the people of the east, and all the wisdom of Egypt" (1 Kings 4:30).

The books of Proverbs, Ecclesiastes, Job, and Wisdom provide an extensive range of the proverbial wisdom of Israel, but in this literature the freeing gesture of the Exodus has little part. God is seen as the creator of the natural order and the Supreme One behind the moral order of human relationships. This wisdom, the ability to discern or judge what is true and right, is the result of keenly observing God's creation—the arrangement of the stars, the seasons of the year, and order in social life. Thus Proverbs declares that "the fear of the Lord prolongs life, but the years of the wicked will be short" (Prov 10:27). The writer observes that a well-ordered life results in good health and long life; wickedness—that is, the failure to follow God's rules—leads to a shameful life.[21] In the Book of Wisdom, true wisdom is acting justly and compassionately no matter how old or young we may be:

> The upright, though he die before his time,
>   will find rest.
> Length of days is not what makes age hon-
>   orable,
> nor number of years the true measure of
>   life;
> understanding, this is grey hairs,

---

[21] See Walter Brueggemann, *Disruptive Grace: Reflections on God, Scripture, and the Church*, ed. Carolyn J. Sharp (Minneapolis: Fortress Press, 2011), 251.

untarnished life, this is ripe old age. (Wis
4:7–9, NJB).

Understanding in this text means the ability to ponder
one's personal experience and the Israelite experience
and to act on their lessons; this is something that people
must constantly work at. It is a quality that can be taught
but, more important, it is a human quality that can be
achieved by contemplating the lives of people like Joseph
and Solomon, as is evident in the books of Proverbs and
Ecclesiastes. This contemplation, however, is a gift of God,
not something attainable by human effort alone: "For Wisdom . . . is a breath of the power of God, pure emanation of
the glory of the Almighty; . . . untarnished mirror of God's
active power, and image of his goodness" (Wis 7:25–26).
In these books the wisdom tradition is "an ongoing reflective conversation in which different interpreters proposed
different instructional judgments" and these "judgments
were to some extent open, ready to be revised in the face
of continuing experience."[22] Thus, for instance, according
to Proverbs, elderly people with gray hair have honor only
if they give good example to the young: "Gray hair is a
crown of glory; it is gained in a righteous life" (Prov 16:31).
Through praiseworthy actions the elderly help to educate
the young: "Train children in the right way, and when old,
they will not stray" (Prov 22:6).

Aging and Death

Death is a fact of life to the Israelites, the normal consequence of being a creature of God: "The Lord gave, and

---

[22] Brueggemann, *Reverberations of Faith*, 234.

the Lord has taken away; blessed is the name of the Lord" (Job 1:21). There is no attempt to deny the inevitability and total finality of death; God alone is immortal (Ps 90:1–6). The insight that death is related to sin is to be found in Genesis 2:17 and Wisdom 1:12–16, but this point remains somewhat underdeveloped throughout the Old Testament. After death the deceased continued to exist in some temporary, nondynamic, or passive way in Sheol, though from time to time there are some very faint expressions of hope that death is not the end of life (see Ps 73:23–28). What is of crucial importance to the Israelites is this: the deceased is only a human being whose life has value not in terms of any afterlife, but simply in terms of the way it has been lived. The wise Israelite would ponder the inevitability of death, not as a reminder to prepare for the afterlife, but as an incentive to live life according to the covenant requirements of God (Ps 90:12).

A death was considered good if certain conditions had been fulfilled: the normal life span of 120 years according to Genesis 6:3, 70 years according to Psalm 90:10; many children to carry on one's name; and evidence that one has lived in the service of God. There is reason to mourn without restraint if sickness, disaster, or sinful action threatens to cut short an individual's or the nation's life. The person or nation can do nothing from the grave (Ps 103:15–16). The fear of losing contact with God's believing and worshiping community through death becomes increasingly evident, as Walther Eichrodt notes, as Israelites become more knowledgeable about what is meant by the covenant community. The loss of one's links with the community destroys one's identity and union with God.[23] If premature death is likely,

---

[23] See Walther Eichrodt, *The Theology of the Old Testament* (London: SCM Press, 1967), 497–529.

then the true Israelite would remind God that the dead can no longer be present with the living to worship him: "Do you work wonders for the dead? Do the shades rise up to praise you?" (Ps 88:10).

Job and Wisdom

My days are past, my plans are broken off, the desires of my heart.

—Job 17:11

The story of the aging Job is a fine reminder that human pondering on events of life is ultimately limited. Without faith that comes from God, no amount of contemplation on one's declining years can achieve true wisdom. The Book of Job, surely one of the world's finest pieces of literature, is about the sufferings of innocent people in their journey of life.[24] Many Israelites believe that Yahweh rewards the righteous with material well-being, as the book of Proverbs asserts (1:32; 3:1–2, 13–18; 8:36), but this contradicts the experience of many god-fearing people, including Job. The author examines the problem presented in story form and in a series of poems, and he ventures some new wise solutions to the puzzling issue. William Whedbee has cogently argued that the book contains at least two central features of comedy: its perception of incongruity, and a basic plot line that finally evokes a surprising and energizing joy for

---

[24] See Gerald A. Arbuckle, *Change, Grief, and Renewal in the Church: A Spirituality for a New Era* (Westminster, MD: Christian Classics, 1991), 76–78. For commentaries see J. E. Hartley, *The Book of Job* (Grand Rapids, MI: Eerdmans, 1988); J. G. Janzen, "Job," in *Interpretation: A Bible Commentary for Teaching and Preaching* (Atlanta: John Knox Press, 1985); M. H. Pope, *Job* (New York: Doubleday, 1965).

Job and his return to a harmonious society.[25] The playwright Christopher Fry makes the same claim. He speaks of Job as "the great reservoir of comedy."[26]

The journey of Job into the authentic wisdom of following God's will can be divided into three stages. In the first stage Job is depicted as the model of the righteous man and, therefore, according to Jewish beliefs at that time, his human successes are God's rewards; he is blessed with many children, good health, social respectability, and large flocks and herds. He has shown justice and compassion to widows, orphans, and strangers, that is, toward people especially loved by God but marginalized by Israelite society. For him, everything flourishes. Then disasters begin to hit, including the development of loathsome sores "from the sole to his head" (Job 2:7), but his reaction is one of calm acceptance and patience. He receives no support from his wife, who demands that he should curse God and die (Job 2:9). He refuses to change his attitude: "You speak as a foolish woman. . . . Shall we receive the good at the hand of God, and not receive the bad?" (Job 2:10). The storyteller is indicating to listeners that a paradox is about to be presented to them.

The second stage of his journey, which is described in chapters 3—42, is the contemplative one. It is a contest between two types of wisdom: the wisdom of the world and the wisdom of God. Job struggles to make sense of what has happened. His three friends sit with him, silently contemplating Job's catastrophes, believing they are all in retribution for Job's sinfulness. His secure world has disintegrated. He loses wealth, health, and family. His whole herd is stolen; his children are killed; and he is covered

---

[25] See William Whedbee, "The Comedy of Job," ed. Robert Polzin and David Robertson, *Semeia* 7 (1977): 1–44.

[26] Christopher Fry, as quoted in ibid., 32.

with bleeding sores. No one will approach him for fear of catching the disease. The rubbish dump where he sits and the sores that he pitifully scratches with some broken pottery are vivid symbols of his personal chaos. Job breaks down, cursing the day he was born (Job 3). He laments his desperate loneliness and his abandonment by God: "So I am allotted months of emptiness and nights of misery are apportioned to me" (Job 7:3). "I say to the Pit, 'You are my Father', and to the worm, 'My mother' or 'My sister' . . . where then is my hope?" (Job 17:11, 14, 15).

Here is the paradox that troubles Job in the depth of his heart. He has done all the right things, despite the protestations to the contrary from his friends, yet he is being punished by God. Puzzled by this incongruous situation, Job says to God: "If I sin, what do I do to you, you watcher of humanity? Why have you made me your target? Why have I become a burden to you?" (Job 7:20). He gazes nostalgically back to his years of prosperity. His wife encourages him to curse God, and his friends berate him and accuse him of insulting God, but Job continues to call on God who now seems utterly inaccessible and uninterested in his plight: "Oh, that I knew where I might find him, that I might come even to his dwelling!" (Job 23:3).

Yet, in the midst of his darkness, so like the dark night of the soul as described by Saint John of the Cross,[27] Job still has energizing hope, and this is the third stage of his journey: "For I know that my Redeemer lives, and that at the last he will stand upon the earth; and after my skin has been thus destroyed, then in my flesh I shall see God, whom I shall see on my side" (Job 19:25, 27). Having mourned his grief, Job is open to hear God's response to the bewildering mystery of evil. The world, Job discovers, is alive with the

---

[27] See Chapter 5 herein.

mystery of God's wisdom. In spite of what Job or others might think, God is in charge, and God holds all creation together. There is to be no return to primeval chaos. Job is reassured that God cares for him far more than for all the animals. His sufferings have befallen him in line with God's wisdom, the same wisdom that allows Job to have good health and material prosperity (Job 38:1—40:2; 40:6—41:32).

Human reason alone is powerless to understand evil; only faith in God makes evil bearable. The ultimate measure for judging whether or not people are devout is the moral quality of their lives and not the fortuitous status of their material wealth.[28] The incongruous situation that Job was grappling with from the beginning of the narrative is resolved in a way unimagined by human reason. Peace enters Job's soul. Gifted with this wisdom Job concludes his spiritual journey with an inspiring prayer of humility, inner joy, tranquillity, and thanks: "I know that you can do all things, and that no purpose of yours can be thwarted. . . . I had heard of you by the hearing of the ear, but now my eye sees you; therefore I despise myself, and repent in dust and ashes" (Job 42:2, 5). The fact that his material prosperity is restored to him is insignificant when compared to his newfound wisdom.

The lesson that Job learned remains universally relevant. Like Job, we, young or old, are called to abandon our entire selves to God's all-embracing wisdom and love. It is to be hoped that God will give us the same surprising, invigorating gift of new insight and consolation: "I have uttered what I did not understand, things too wonderful for me, which I did not know" (Job 42:3). No longer does his heart faint within him (Job 19:27).

---

[28] See David J. Clines, "The Book of Job," in *The Oxford Companion to the Bible,* ed. Bruce M. Metzger and Michael D. Coogan (New York: Oxford University Press, 1993), 370.

New Testament: Aging, Wisdom, and Death

> *For God's foolishness is wiser than human wisdom, and God's weakness is stronger than human strength.*
>
> —1 Corinthians 1:25

Two basic themes in Saint Paul's letters are the need to become a new creation through baptism and the wisdom that must guide every aspect of life in consequence of this creation. He writes: "So if anyone is in Christ, there is a new creation: everything old has passed away; see, everything has become new!" (2 Cor 5:17). Created anew through Christ's redemptive power, our task is to struggle throughout our mortal life, despite our aging bodies, to witness to the power of Christ through love and justice. With Christ we say: "We must work the works of him who sent me while it is day; night is coming when no one can work" (John 9:4). Paul speaks of Christ as "the wisdom of God" (1 Cor 1:24), and for that reason Christ is in the journey of life "the way, and the truth, and the life" (John 14:6). What he teaches and lives is *the* wise way to God at every stage of life's journey. What Christ does are the works of wisdom (Matt 11:18–19). "Learn from me; for I am gentle and humble in heart, and you will find rest for your souls" (Matt 11:29). From Christ we learn that no matter how old and infirm we may be we can still witness to Christ's life within us. We can unite our very sufferings with those of Christ: "Rejoice in hope, be patient in suffering, persevere in prayer" (Rom 12:12).

In the New Testament wisdom, following the Old Testament wisdom tradition, is also a human quality as we see Jesus' interactions with the Pharisees when he challenges them to understand what an ordered life demands and allows (Mark 12:13–37). In his parables we see the same dynamic at work as he aims to stimulate people in an inductive way to think about how they should behave. Ultimately, however, true wisdom comes from acknowledging that Jesus Christ—living, dying on the cross, and rising—*is* wisdom. This is a gift of faith that God alone can give through the Spirit. Several figures in the New Testament offer examples of grace-filled aging and wisdom.

- Mary, who puts aside her human fears of the unknown, accepts in faith the call of God to be the mother of the messiah (Luke 1:26–38); as she ages, her faith is rewarded with an ever-deepening gift of wisdom. This is evident at the crucifixion scene. One can picture Mary, possibly about fifty years old, clinging to Jesus, not wishing him to die (John 19:25–26). Yet she painfully and in faith assents to his death. She mourns his passing and receives a new role: "Woman, here is your son" (John 19:26). Now she is to be the mother of all who come to believe in Jesus down through the ages. In the midst of her grief she is to be the support and model of detachment of every gospel community that yearns to love Jesus and to lament over its own failings and sinfulness.[29]
- The childless Zachary, when told that he and his aging wife would have a son, did not believe the angel Gabriel: "I am an old man, and my wife is getting on in years" (Luke 1:18). Because of his lack of faith Zachary became "mute, unable to speak" (Luke 1:20). Human wisdom made no sense of the angel's message, but when his son was born "his mouth was opened and his tongue freed, and he began to speak, praising God"

---

[29] Arbuckle, *Laughing with God*, 85.

(v. 64). Then Zachary, now "filled with the Holy Spirit" (v. 67)—the source of all wisdom—spoke one of the most dignified songs of praise of the entire scriptures, "bringing together into a few lines many of the most powerful themes in Israel's prophetic heritage."[30]

- There is Joseph, foster-father of Jesus. Matthew's account of the birth of Jesus describes the wisdom of a man struggling to discover how to relate justly with the surprising pregnancy of his fiancée (Matt 1:18–25) and how to react to the dangers faced by the infant Jesus (Matt 2:13–23). Human wisdom alone could not help him, but only the wisdom that comes from God. Thus he acted with faith-inspired integrity: "He did as the angel of the Lord commanded him" (Matt 1:24). As the child whom Joseph protected grew, he "increased in wisdom and in years, and in divine and human favor" (Luke 2:52), no doubt influenced by the wisdom of both his father and his mother.

- The elderly Anna, "a widow to the age of eighty-four" (Luke 2:37), and Simeon also model for us the wisdom of prayerful aging that is open to the Spirit and gazes hopefully to the future. Under the guidance of the Holy Spirit they foretell the blessings that will come to the nations through the birth of Jesus Christ but also note that there will be sufferings ahead for Mary, the child's mother: "A sword will pierce your own soul too" (Luke 2:35). Anna had been in the Temple, where she "worshiped there with fasting and prayer night and day" (Luke 2:37), a sure reminder that the wisdom of aging can be achieved not by human means alone.

---

[30] Samuel O. Abogunrin, "Luke," in *The International Bible Commentary*, ed. William R. Farmer (Collegeville, MN: Liturgical Press, 1998), 1375.

- The parable of the dysfunctional family (normally referred to as the parable of the prodigal son) contains
wonderful lessons of how an aging wise father should
react to intergenerational tensions (Luke 15:11–32).[31]
First, there is the narcissistic behavior of the rebellious
adolescent who squanders his inheritance on "dis-
solute living" (Luke 15:13). He eventually and wisely,
by reflecting on his experience of life, acknowledges
his stupidity and is transformed into a caring son of
a sorrowing father. The elder son selfishly refuses to
console and support his father because he rejects his
role as an intermediary between his wayward brother
and his father, and he also fails to be hospitable to
guests. But his aging father, who has been gravely
and publicly shamed by both his sons, yearns to be
reconciled with them. Although humanly speaking he
has every reason to continue to reject his younger son,
the father is quick to receive him. He "was filled with
compassion; he ran and put his arms around him and
kissed him" (Luke 15:20). He is an example of wisdom
acquired over decades of self-reflection on the experience of life. The envious and jealous elder son refuses
the offer for reunion (Luke 15:25–32), but his father still
hopes for reconciliation. The young man fails to heed
the example of the wisdom of his father.
- Saint Paul sees life's journey as a process of ongoing
spiritual incidents of dying and rising, of dying to
selfishness and rising in Christ (Phil 1:21); to do this
we must become "fools for the sake of Christ" (1 Cor
4:10), and this is true wisdom. The message of Christ
by worldly standards is incongruous: "For the message about the cross is foolishness to those who are

---

[31] See Arbuckle, *Laughing with God*, 78–80.

perishing, but to us who are being saved it is the power of God" (1 Cor 1:18). In a satirical way Paul says: "For Jews demand signs and the Greeks desire wisdom, but we proclaim Christ crucified, a stumbling block to Jews and foolishness to Gentiles" (1 Cor 1:22–23). He then explains why in worldly terms Christ's message is nonsense. Christ bypasses those with power and embraces the weak; powerlessness is the model of true power and foolishness becomes the wisdom of God: "But God chose what is foolish in the world to shame the wise; God chose what is weak in the world to shame the strong; God chose what is low and despised in the world, things that are not, to reduce to nothing things that are, so that no one might boast in the presence of God" (1 Cor 1:27–29). Paul asks the Corinthians to reflect on the paradox of his own life. They know his many weaknesses, yet the power of God shines through (2 Cor 12:10).[32]

A sign of authentic wisdom is laughter of the heart. Laughter of the heart is the inner joy and peace that God alone can give through the power of his death and resurrection: "By his great mercy he has given us a new birth into a living hope through the resurrection of Jesus Christ from the dead, and into an inheritance that is imperishable, undefiled, and unfading, kept in heaven for you" (1 Pet 1:3–4). It is this peace that "surpasses all understanding" (Phil 4:7). In the resurrection God is laughing at death, so that with Paul we can say: "Death has been swallowed up in victory. Where, O death, is your victory? Where, O death, is your sting" (1 Cor 15:54–55). Paul at one point ponders how the face of the risen Christ reflects that glory of the creator God:

---

[32] See ibid., 89–90.

"For it is the God who said, 'Let light shine out of the darkness,' who has shone in our hearts to give the light of the knowledge of the glory of God in the face of Jesus Christ" (2 Cor 4:6). Paul's heart is so transformed by this same light that he could exclaim: "I have been crucified with Christ; and it is no longer I who live, but it is Christ who lives in me" (Gal 2:19–20).

Care for Aging People

The wisdom of God can conflict with the wisdom of the world. In biblical times people depended for their identity, housing, and food on their kinship system. However, there was a seriously negative side to this custom: people felt no obligation to assist anyone outside their kinship system. This was contrary to the fundamental commandment to love one another and show compassion to anyone in need (Luke 10:25–37). This meant, however, that followers of Christ risked expulsion from their kinship system when they went to the aid of a non-kinsman in need.[33] Jesus is referring to this when he says, "Do not think that I have come to bring peace to the earth; I have not come to bring peace, but a sword; . . . one's foes will be members of one's own household" (Matt 10:34, 36). Jesus hints at this tension also when he responds to the summons from "his mother and his brothers" to come to them (Mark 3:31). He replies that ultimate identity and support will not come from traditional extended family systems but from their faith communities: "Here are my mother and my brothers! Whoever does the will of God is my brother and sister and mother" (Mark 3:35).

---

[33] See Neyrey, "Loss of Wealth, Loss of Family, Loss of Honor," 100–101.

Elderly people, therefore, who had been rejected by their kinsfolk because they had become followers of Christ would indeed have been placed in very difficult circumstances. Consequently, it is not surprising that early converts very quickly "had all things in common; they would sell their possessions and goods and distribute the proceeds to all, as any had need" (Acts 2:44–45). These early Christians gradually formed "a miniature welfare state in an empire which for the most part lacked social services," a system based on need, not on whether or not people belonged to particular kinship systems.[34] The faith communities, when necessary, would assume the responsibilities of the kinship system, caring for "widows and orphans, the old, the unemployed, and the disabled."[35]

This principle does not mean that our obligations to kinsfolk cease if they are in need. Saint Paul explicitly and in strong language reminds the early Christians to take care of their relatives, especially "family members." Whoever fails to do this "has denied the faith and is worse than an unbeliever" (1 Tim 5:8). By "family members" Paul is referring to the household, which included grandparents as well as younger relatives. Paul opens his section of his letter by reminding Christians "not to speak harshly to an older man, but to speak to him as to a father . . . to older women as mothers" (1 Tim 5:1–2). According to Paul, following the teaching of Christ means that concern for the aging must extend beyond one's relatives. Elsewhere he writes: "So then, whenever we have an opportunity, let us work for the good of all, and especially for those of the family of faith"

---

[34] Paul Johnson, cited in Gary B. Ferngreen, *Medicine and Health Care in Early Christianity* (Baltimore: Johns Hopkins University Press, 2009), 138.

[35] Ferngreen, *Medicine and Health Care in Early Christianity*, 139.

(Gal 6:10); baptism makes us into a kind of family, a family bonded together in faith. At the same time, however, Paul is at pains to tell Christians that the bonds among all Christians, including the relationship between the young and old—no matter whether they are biologically related or not—should be charity: "Love is patient; love is kind; . . . And now faith, hope, and love abide, these three; and the greatest of these is love" (1 Cor 13:4, 13); "Owe no one anything, except to love one another; for the one who loves another has fulfilled the law" (Rom 13:8).

Gospel Wisdom and Death

The wisdom of Christ is also strikingly evident in the way death at any age is to be perceived. Death for the believing Christian, contrary to pagan understanding, is not the end of life. Physically, yes, but through the resurrection of Christ our lives are spiritually transformed. Saint Paul likens our human bodies to a tent. He knew, and his desert listeners would have readily understood, that a tent is easy to fold up, to pack away. Travelers can then move to a better place in their journey. But there is a major problem with living in a tent, Paul says. It can be a fragile home. It can suddenly be blown away by a storm, or it can wear out. While we live in our earthly tents, Paul says, "we groan, longing to be clothed with our heavenly dwelling. . . . For while we are still in this tent, we groan under our burden, because we wish not to be unclothed but to be further clothed, so that what is mortal may be swallowed up by life" (2 Cor 5:2, 4). Through our faith we know that in leaving this world behind we can move permanently to our true home in heaven with Jesus Christ: "It is God who has designed this for us for this very purpose. . . . We are always full of confidence, then, realizing that as long as we are at home in the tent of our body, we are exiled from the Lord. . . . We long to be exiled from the body to be at home with the Lord." This world is but a stage toward this haven of peace: "What no eye has seen and no ear has heard, what the mind of man cannot visualize; all that God has prepared for those who love him" (1 Cor 2:9).

In brief, the wisdom of Christ teaches us that physical death is a reality, but it denies it is the end of life. Death is the beginning of new life in Christ. "But we do not want you to be uninformed . . . about those who have died, so that you may not grieve as others do who have no hope. For since we believe that Jesus died and rose again, even so, through Jesus God will bring with him those who have died" (1 Thess 4:13–14).

Summary

- Many incidents in the scriptures describe the symptoms of personal and collective or national aging and its many losses and sorrows, death being its ultimate conclusion.
- The Israelites are the people of God. In return for God's creative love the Israelites must act justly toward one another and strangers; when they forget the wisdom message they are overwhelmed by chaos and its terrifying expressions. If, however, the Israelites admit they are lost and desperately need God's forgiving presence, they experience a newness and vitality no matter how old they may be biologically.
- Psalms 71 and 90, in particular, focus on the challenges of personal and collective aging; for example, the fear that God will desert the Israelites in their old age. Despite their depression, however, God-given

wisdom assures them that God will never leave them. This wisdom is contrary to worldly people, like Job's friends, who judge events only in terms of their limited human insights.

- In the New Testament true wisdom comes from acknowledging that Jesus Christ *is* wisdom itself; by faith we share in this wisdom. No matter how old we might be biologically, this wisdom gives us an inner youthfulness. In imitation of Christ's life, death, and resurrection, this wisdom motivates us to keep struggling compassionately and justly toward our neighbors to the moment we die. Then "he will wipe every tear from [our] eyes. Death will be no more; mourning and crying and pain will be no more, for the first things have passed away" (Rev 21:4).

- Fundamental message: the pilgrimage of life calls us to let go of false attachments and to be open to God's will. The more we are truly pilgrim people, the more we will rediscover the inner power of God's energizing love: "For to me, living is Christ and dying is gain" (Phil 1:21). This is true wisdom.

2

Aging in Cultures

The Universal Call to Let Go

*As the older person moves toward un-
explored boundaries, he or she is called
upon to create new models for living.
Precedents for creative aging amid
modern uncertainties are lacking. Thus
the most disturbing of times can become a season for innovative ventures.*
— EUGENE C. BIANCHI,
AGING AS A SPIRITUAL JOURNEY, 144-45

*Crabbed age and youth cannot live to-
gether: Youth is full of pleasance, age
is full of care.*
— ATTRIBUTED TO WILLIAM SHAKESPEARE

Key points covered in this chapter

- There is no universally accepted definition of old age.

- Western and traditional cultures relate to the issues of aging in different ways.
- Aging people in all cultures have the challenge to discover ways to relinquish attachments to the past in order to be able to move forward.
- Masters of the spiritual life suggest various approaches to guide people to receive God-given youthfulness.

No unanimous definitions of what it means to be young or old exist. But whatever definitions are chosen, one thing is universally true: to move from being young to old while remaining youthful in spirit requires the art of relinquishing attachments to times past. It calls for a process of mourning. This chapter has two aims. The first is to review sociologically the different approaches in Western and traditional cultures to aging. However, these cultures are no longer geographically neatly separated. Through widespread migration from Asia, the Middle East, and the South Pacific Islands to Europe, North America, and Australasia, traditional cultures are increasingly part of Western societies. The Catholic Church's 2014 Synod on the Family invited us to identify family pastoral challenges, including issues of aging, giving added relevance to this chapter. The second aim is to explain briefly what Saint Teresa of Avila suggests are ways to let go those attachments that hinder or stop people, at any age, from receiving God-given youthfulness.

Definitions of aging depend very much on the culture people belong to and how they individually view life. Recently I was having difficulties parking my small car outside a busy shopping center. My admittedly slow movements aroused the anger of a well-dressed young man in an expensive BMW who was unable to pass me. In rather colorful language he shouted at me: "You old gray-haired <bleep>. It's time you were pensioned off and off the <bleep> road!" For a moment my self-confidence and self-esteem were shaken. By his estimate, and the commonly accepted attitudes of people in his culture, I was so old, as indicated by my gray hair and slow movements, that I should be confined to a rest home, hidden from society, with reduced claims to conventional adult status. What a contrast with my experience in the traditional culture of Samoa in the South Pacific! There my gray hair and wrinkles are presumed to be symbols of wisdom, demanding deep respect from younger members of the community.

Aging in Western Societies

In the Western world, people are generally labeled aging or old for two reasons: they receive financial support from the state, and/or they have visible signs that are associated with aging, such as gray hair and wrinkles. These classifications are oversimplified, however, because the literature on aging is filled with a great variety of often controversial definitions. For example, in an effort to separate old age from eligibility for a state pension and its derogatory association with dependency in Australia, "from 1997 onwards much of the policy literature has used the age of 50 as the 'start' of old age."[1] Health and social services, on the other hand, commonly select a biological age after which social and treatment needs are dispensed by different specialist categories. Consequently, there are geriatricians, medical consultants who deal specifically with older clients, and specialist nurses and social workers who care for older people.

---

[1] Alan Walker and Tony Maltby, "Older People," in *The Student's Companion to Social Policy*, ed. Pete Alcock, Margaret May, and Karen Rowlingson (Oxford: Blackwell Publishing, 2008), 395.

However, since the average age of death continues to rise, chronological age indicators are not truly satisfactory. Therefore, sociologists keep devising new categories to define what old age involves. For example, sociologist Jane Pilcher describes four stages of life: the *first age*, childhood, which is the time of dependency and socialization; the *second age,* a time of full employment, building a family, and adult responsibilities; the *third age,* the "new middle age" (between fifty and seventy-four), the period of active independent life, grandparenting, and eventual retirement from full-time work; and the *fourth age,* which is specifically old age (seventy-five and older) and is noted by Pilcher for its increasing dependence on others.[2] Unfortunately, once people reach this fourth age, the tendency in society is to treat them as dependent and mentally weakened even if they are not. Some refer to people over eighty-five, the fastest-growing section of the population in Western societies, as the "oldest old." The division sometimes implies that the "young old" are active while the "old old" are passive and dependent, but this distinction is gravely inaccurate; research in Britain and other EU countries shows quite a different conclusion. An increasing number of "old old" people are not passive and dependent. Indeed, persons over eighty sometimes refer to old age as "ten years older than I am."

---

[2] See Jane L. Pilcher, *Age and Generation in Modern Britain* (Oxford: Oxford University Press, 1995). Postmodern theorists are uncomfortable with the use of the term *stages of life* because they want to avoid any language that assumes the stages are biologically determined or permanent. They prefer the term *life course.* However, "the idea of stages in life [such as young, middle aged, old] is still . . . embedded in ordinary discourse . . . [so] it still makes sociological sense to conceive of stages in the life course" (James Fulcher and John Scott, *Sociology* [Oxford: Oxford University Press, 2007], 453–54).

Ageism

Ageism describes the negative stereotyping of and/or discrimination against people by reason of their age. The victims may be young or old. In the Western world, in which youth is exalted, the mass media encourage images of older people that are outdated, discourteous, and often ludicrous. Older people are stereotyped as lonely, unable to learn, in poor health, and dependent on others.[3] They are expected to behave according to these images, and they commonly suffer work discrimination as a consequence.[4] Robert Butler concludes that ageism "allows the young generations to see older people as different from themselves, thus they subtly cease to identify with their elders as human beings."[5] Older people may lose adult titles, like Ms., Mrs., or Mr., and be summoned by their Christian names (like children) "or given diminutive titles like 'dear' or 'love.'"[6]

Little wonder that the self-esteem of aging people is undermined by this nasty stereotyping. The fact is that most older people remain active, relishing their independence, and often provide significant assistance within families, such as child care, or continuing paid employment, if

---

[3] See Christina Victor, *The Social Context of Ageing* (London: Routledge, 2005).

[4] In Britain 60 percent of older people agree that age discrimination exists in their daily lives and 53 percent of adults agree that people treat those in old age as children (see "Later Life in the United Kingdom" [June 2013], available—and updated monthly—on the ageuk.org.uk website). John Paul II writes of the social exclusion of elderly people in his 1981 apostolic exhortation *On the Role of the Christian Family (Familiaris Consortia),* no. 41.

[5] Robert Butler, *Why Survive? Being Old in America* (New York: Harper and Row, 1975), 35.

[6] Mike Featerstone and Mike Hepworth, "Images of Ageing: Cultural Representations of Later Life," in *The Cambridge Handbook of Age and Ageing,* ed. Malcolm L. Johnson (Cambridge: Cambridge University Press, 2005), 358.

possible (many countries insist on compulsory retirement at sixty-five and/or employers discriminate against older people).[7] Unfortunately, since the emphasis in Western societies is focused on young people, sociologists have for the most part given insufficient time to studying aging and old age, however they are defined.

Theories of Aging

Western sociologists have formulated a variety of some-times conflicting theories of aging and the role of older people in society, theories that further illustrate just how difficult it is for commentators to agree on definitions. Theories of aging include the following, which are discussed below: role, disengagement, dependency, social inequality, feminist, and positive.[8] The *role theory* assumes that chronological age determines certain behaviors; all older people are assumed to want to retire from work or live in retirement homes at a certain age. The *disengagement* theory asserts that older people are medically weak, and society should arrange for them to retire from work at a certain age. This theory has definite objectives: first, it allows younger people to take over positions of responsibility; second, it provides the chance for organizations to acknowledge through the ritual of a retirement farewell the achievements of the person leaving employment; and third, it presumes that new and dynamic ideas will replace out-dated ones. However, research has shown—contrary to the

---

[7] See Victor, *The Social Context of Ageing*, 400.

[8] I summarize below the helpful analyses by Lorne Tepperman and Josh Curtis, *Social Problems: A Canadian Perspective* (Don Mills: Oxford University Press, 2011), 150–69; and Margaret Sargent, Pamela Nilan, and Gabriele Winter, *The New Sociology for Australians* (South Melbourne: Longman, 1997), 180–89.

negative stereotype that older workers have lower capacity to learn new methods and jobs than younger workers—that learning capacity generally does not show any noticeable decline before the age of seventy.[9] The *dependency* theory assumes that older people develop dependency traits as the natural consequence of aging. Once people are classified as old, they tend to be treated as dependent, and as physically and mentally incapacitated, irrespective of their characteristics as individuals. This theory fails to recognize that dependency is often caused by social and structural pressures; for example, low financial resources may force individuals, including some older people, to develop dependency attitudes just to survive.

Other theories question the validity of the assumptions behind these theories. The *social inequality* theory claims that mandatory retirement and downsizing policies are basically strategies to achieve more profits at the expense of older workers, who are thought to be closed to innovation. But when older people do disengage and withdraw from society, it is often because social pressures force them to do so, not because they can't deal with new ideas. The *feminist* theory assumes that older women are more pressured than men to retire because aging for women is commonly associated with the loss of physical attractiveness. The *political* theory argues that since older people have little or no political power base, their voices are not heard; this theory blames the media and other social pressures that hide the creative gifts of many older people. It is, however, losing its validity as the Baby Boomers, who are vocal in Western societies, edge toward old age.

The *positive* theory is particularly critical of the negative Western stereotypical assumptions about aging. It does

---

[9] See Taylor Cox, *Cultural Diversity in Organizations: Theory, Research, and Practice* (San Francisco: Berrett-Koehler, 1994), 90.

not deny that aging brings challenges. Above all, positive theorists point out that older people are a diverse group with vastly different needs and capacities. They do not form a homogenous mass, and their needs must not be evaluated solely in economic terms. The fact is that many older people are engaged in unpaid and voluntary work of a vital nature. Michael Coory, writing in *The Medical Journal of Australia,* summarizes research into the needs of older people in Australia: "Numerous studies have shown that the effect of population ageing on health expenditure is likely to be small and manageable." He significantly adds that "pessimistic scenarios have stifled debate and limited the number of policy options considered."[10]

Older People: Losses and Griefs

Older people in Western societies experience numerous losses such as social and economic losses associated with retirement from work; loss of spouses and friends; increasing isolation as family members marry and move elsewhere; lost opportunities to change decisions about life; and loss of independence because of physical and/or mental health problems. All these factors can evoke within older people an increasing sense of diminishment as persons, with their loss of self-esteem and self-respect intensified by socially constructed negative stereotyping. Hence, the more we can appreciate the grief and mourning involved in many of the changes that elderly people must undergo, the better

---

[10] Michael D. Coory, "Ageing and Healthcare Costs in Australia: A Case of Policy-based Evidence?" www.mja.com.au. *The Economist* cautiously argues against accepting without question "the dire warnings about the bankrupting consequences of a 'grey tusunami'" in economically developed countries ("Age Invaders" [April 26, 2014]: 20).

prepared we are to grasp the complex adjustments they are called to make. Perhaps the most difficult interconnected challenges for older people are, first, to let the past go, leaving space to identify gratefully the good things they have been able to achieve and to forgive themselves for the mistakes they have made and the hurts they have caused others over years, a process bringing peace of mind and heart;[11] and second, the need to find ways in which their self-esteem and self-respect can be maintained. Not an easy set of challenges! William Wordsworth (1770–1850) wrote: "The wiser mind mourns less for what age takes away, than what it leaves behind." How true!

Aging and Wisdom: Secular Insights

Aristotle conceived of wisdom as something essentially practical. For him, practical wisdom as a virtue requires knowing, in general, how to live well.[12] At one point he considered "the various types of human character, in relation to the emotions and moral qualities, showing how they correspond to various ages."[13] Aristotle thought that the journey of life is divided into three stages: the young, the middle aged, and the elderly.[14] For him the young and elderly faced the most difficulties in developing practical wisdom. The young are given to excesses; they are over-confident, they lack experience, they tend to see the good

---

[11] See Gerald M. Fagin, "The Spiritual Exercises and the Later Years," *The Way* 43/1 (January 2004): 70.

[12] See Aristotle, *Nichomachean Ethics,* VI, trans. W. Rhys Roberts, ed. Robert M. Hutchins, *Great Books of the Western World*, vol. 9 (Chicago: Encyclopaedia Britannica, 1952), 1140a-b.

[13] Aristotle, *Rhetoric*, in Hutchins, *Great Books of the Western World*, 1388b.

[14] See ibid., 1389a-90b.

in life rather than the bad; they are given to wit which is synonymous with insolence. The elderly, by contrast, have an excess of despair; they have been burned by experience, which results in cynicism and distrustfulness; and they feel only disdain for other people's opinions of them. He wrote bleakly that the elderly are "slaves to the love of gain . . . are querulous, and not disposed to jesting or laughter."[15] The body is in its prime from thirty to thirty-five, and the mind at about fifty. Wisdom, it seems from Aristotle's assessment, is particularly a quality of people in this middle stage of life: "They have neither that excess of confidence which amounts to rashness, nor too much timidity, but the right amount of each. . . . To put it generally . . . all the excesses or defects [of youth and old age] are replaced by moderation and fitness."[16] Fortunately the scriptural insights about wisdom elaborated in the previous chapter critique Aristotle's simplistic view of wisdom.

American psychotherapist Erik Erikson describes eight psychosocial stages of the life cycle. At each stage a person is deeply influenced by physical, biological, social, and intellectual changes, bringing a specific challenge.[17] The seventh stage, which he termed "generativity," is the call to be interested in "establishing and guiding the next generation." Those who fail to develop generativity "often begin to indulge themselves as if they were their own one and only child."[18] Thus generativity demands that people in middle adulthood let go of excessive concern for themselves in

---

[15] Ibid., 1390a.

[16] Ibid., 1390b.

[17] See Erik H. Erikson, *Life Cycle Completed* (New York: W. W. Norton, 1982) and *Insight and Responsibility* (New York: W. W. Norton, 1964), 70.

[18] Erik H. Erikson, *Identity and the Life Cycle* (New York: W. W. Norton, 1980), 103.

order to assist the new generation. Erikson argues that in late adulthood, the time that precedes death, there is the tension between "ego integrity" and "despair." By the former Erikson means that people have the ability to develop a sense of meaning and order, both for themselves and in the way they view their surrounding world. They are able to contemplate their accomplishments and/or failures, forgive themselves and others, and accept death as the completion of life. The ability to do this comes from wisdom. However, if this wisdom is not attained, then people are dissatisfied with their lives and develop despair, often leading to depression and hopelessness in old age.

Aging and Spirituality

Research has shown that there is a positive connection between religiosity/spirituality, well-being and mental health, and physical markers.[19] Australian writer Chris McGillion believes that most people assume spirituality to be "a path to enlightenment that is exciting (as distinct from well-trodden and predictable), intimate (rather than public and thus remote), and informal (which is to say free from rules, regulations and authority)." It has come "to signify everything that religious faith is not."[20] Spirituality in this sense is fast becoming a feature of Western societies separated from religion. Robert Wuthnow of Princeton

---

[19] Alfons Margoen, "Religion, Spirituality, and Older People," in *The Cambridge Handbook of Age and Ageing*, ed. Malcolm L. Johnson (Cambridge: Cambridge University Press, 2005), 368.

[20] Chris McGillion, "Faith, Not Spirituality the Answer," *The Sydney Morning Herald* (February 22, 2000). See also David Tracey, "Contemporary Spirituality," *The Oxford Textbook in Healthcare*, ed. Mark Cobb, Christina M. Puchalski, and Bruce Rumbold (Oxford: Oxford University Press, 2012), 473–79.

University, in his critique of this spirituality independent of religion, notes: "[The movement] should be understood as a distinct product of our times. We want community, but nothing very binding. We want spirituality, but we prefer the sacred to serve us instead of requiring our service."[21] For people who are aging or dying, however, it is very doubtful that this vague expression of spirituality can provide them with the necessary framework in which they can peacefully negotiate the last stages of their lives.[22]

Traditional Cultures: Aging and Tensions

Western categories based on chronological age make no sense in many developing countries where traditional cultures predominate. The Western focus on the nuclear family also is inadequate in these places. When working in Papua New Guinea in the early 1970s, I rarely met people living beyond the biological age of fifty; most would have been classed as old around forty-five. The World Health Organization estimates (2013 data) that the overall life expectancy in Japan is now eighty-four, in Australia eighty-three, in New Zealand eighty-two, in Britain eighty-one, and in the United States eighty. By contrast, in Cameroon sixty one, Nigeria fifty-three, in the Central African Republic forty-nine, and in Sierra Leone forty-eight.[23]

---

[21] Robert Wuthnow, *Sharing the Journey: Support Groups and America's Quest for Community* (New York: Free Press, 1994), 365.

[22] D. Heinz, "Finishing the Story: Aging, Spirituality and the Work of Culture," *Journal of Religious Gerontology* 9/1 (1994): 5.

[23] "WHO Life Expectancy Data by Country," available at https://dl.vecnet.org/files/3197xm05t.

Traditional cultures commonly emphasize harmony, co-hesiveness, togetherness, interdependence, and stability in a kinship group.[24] Kinship does not refer only to members of the nuclear family, with two generations being the norm in Western cultures, but also to members of an extended family consisting of at least three generations. An extended kinship family system, which may spread out to clans and tribes, describes a network of relatives who are connected by marriage or by common descent; all can trace their ancestry back to the same real or mythical person. In Asia, most parts of Africa, and the South Pacific the ideology of the extended kinship family system commonly reigns supreme. One could well describe the Philippines, for example, as "an anarchy of families," and the same description could apply to many Asian or African nations, where "what best serves my family" can be the moral measure of many things.[25] There are rules in kinship systems that determine how people should relate to one another and the sanctions that are imposed if the rules are broken.[26]

The language of kinship—the kinds of relationships that exist among members of kin groups—varies considerably in non-Western societies. Despite these differences certain general axioms describe relationships that affect the position of aging people in a non-Western society. The axioms

---

[24] See Gerald A. Arbuckle, *Violence, Society, and the Church: A Cultural Approach* (Collegeville, MN: Liturgical Press, 2004), 34.

[25] See ibid., 37.

[26] In some tribal cultures, especially in East Africa, central Brazil, and parts of Papua New Guinea, social groupings based on age cut across those based on kinship. Young people, most commonly young men, are grouped together in a named, corporate unit, and as they become older, they remain in the same group. See Roger M. Keesing, *Cultural Anthropology: A Contemporary Perspective* (New York: Holt, Rinehart, and Winston, 1981), 275–78.

also indicate how complex relationships among people of different ages can be in traditional cultures.[27]

Axiom 1: Family identity is more important than individual identity.

The family and kinship relationships are the basic organizing principles of identity and social relationships; this has a profound impact on the ways aging people are regarded. For example, in many countries the family name is placed first; among the Yoruba people of West Africa older people are not referred to by their personal names but with titles such as "the mother of-so-and-so," emphasizing the priority to be given to family identity and obligations.[28] Again, in Fijian villages kinship "terms are preferred to personal names in forms of address."[29] When Matthew wished to define who Jesus was, he started by listing a long genealogy (Matt 1:1–17). Kinship relations are not always based on biological relationships or on marriage; there is also adoptive or fictive kinship, which incorporates an outsider into a kinship network, as is evident also in Matthew's genealogy of Jesus.[30]

---

[27] The documents of Vatican II view the family sociologically only in Western cultural terms; extended family systems and their complexities are overlooked.

[28] See Brian M. Howell and Jennell W. Paris, *Introducing Cultural Anthropology: A Christian Perspective* (Grand Rapids, MI: Baker Academic, 2011), 153.

[29] Ray F. Waters, *Economic Development and Social Change in Fiji* (Oxford: Clarendon Press, 1969), 113.

[30] See F. Scott Spencer, "Those Riotous—Yet Righteous—Foremothers of Jesus: Exploring Matthew's Comic Genealogy," *Are We Amused? Humour About Women in the Biblical Worlds*, ed. Athalya Brenner (London: T and T Clark International, 2003), 7–30.

Axiom 2: Particular family structures determine how younger people should relate to, and call, older members of the extended family.

Two kinship structures are common: *matrilineal* and *patrilineal*. The former means that people trace their ancestry through a female ancestor, the latter, through a male. Among the matrilineal Fox people, Native American Indians, this means that the men of the lineage through three generations are called by a term meaning "mother's brothers," even though some would biologically be of grandfather age. If we look at a man's father's mother's lineage, we see that the women are called grandmother, though only one of them would be the man's biological grandmother. It can even happen that a "grandmother" is chronologically younger than the "grandchild." Among the North American Hopi Indians, who also have a matrilineal system, all extended-family women of a mother's biological age are called grandmother, and the men are called grandfather.[31]

Allow me to provide an example. While researching economic development in Fiji, South Pacific, I interviewed an Australian manager of a factory complex in Suva, the capital city. He was puzzled: "I have a serious problem. Very commonly men stay away from work because they say their grandmother has died. At first I was understanding, but after a while the same people would come to me again and make the same excuse for their absence. Then I would be angry." In fact, the workers were not deceiving him because sociologically the men have many grandmothers.

---

[31] See G. Duncan Mitchell, *Sociology: The Study of Social Systems* (London: University Tutorial Press, 1959), 60–65.

Axiom 3: Members of kinship groups are united in a network of mutual rights and obligations so that older people have definite roles to play and receive support and respect in return; that is, solidarity, mutuality, and reciprocity are key principles binding kinship groups together.

One fundamental weakness of the Western nuclear family model is that it can be placed under considerable strain emotionally and in other ways because relatives are under no legal or social obligations to assist aging members in times of need. However, in the extended kinship family system, many fathers, mothers, uncles, aunts, and grandparents are ready to assume responsibilities for needy young or older members when those immediately responsible die or are incapacitated. Not infrequently, for example, a person who is injured or insulted by an outsider has the right to call on members of the kinship group for help in seeking revenge or reparation.[32]

Axiom 4: Unlike Western cultures, traditional cultures normally require younger people to show significant respect for older kinship members.

Simply stated, sociologically defined grandparents and grandchildren generally mutually relate to one another in an unrestrained and friendly manner; on the other hand, parents relate to their children with sternness. The friendliness shown by grandchildren to their grandparents, and to older people in general, is a form of respect, so it must not descend into abuse.[33] On the other hand, anthropologist

---

[32] See Garry W. Trompf, *Payback: The Logic of Retribution in Melanesian Religions* (Cambridge: Cambridge University Press, 1994), 23–96.

[33] See Douglas L. Oliver, *A Solomon Island Society: Kinship and Leadership among the Siuai of Bougainvile* (Cambridge: Harvard University Press, 1955), 271.

Jared Diamond notes some traditional cultures "accord their elderly even lower status than do Americans, starving or abandoning or actively killing them."[34]

The Siuai

The Siuai tribal people of matrilineal descent reside in a remote part of the developing country of Papua New Guinea on the island of Bougainville. The basic social unit is the household that consists of a nuclear family, but members of the extended family will live only meters away. This proximity encourages married children to visit their parents very frequently, especially as parents approach senility. While age itself does not command great respect, their adult offspring are usually tenderly affectionate toward aging parents, demonstrating by word and deed that they feel an obligation for their welfare. As it is explained by one informant: "When we were children they fed and cared for us well; and now that they are aged we repay by giving food to them. For, if we did not, they would surely starve" (Oliver, A Solomon Island Society, 209).

In summary, the reciprocity of social relationships is commonly a fundamental reality of kinship systems.[35] There will be *many* people having the titles grandparent and grandchild, though they may not be biologically related. The titles connote mutual obligations of support and care. By contrast, in Western societies a grandchild, if he or she is lucky, has two sets of grandparents and there are no social and legal obligations for mutual support and care. The

---

[34] Jared Diamond, *The World Until Yesterday* (London: Allen Lane, 2013), 21.
[35] See Joy Hendry, *An Introduction to Social Anthropology: Other People's Worlds* (Basingstoke: Macmillan Press, 1999), 56–59.

nuclear family is centered on domestic needs and held together by close emotional relationships that extend beyond its boundaries to older relations only by choice.

Axiom 5: When traditional cultures increasingly interact with Western cultures, aging people experience significant losses of status and support; in the midst of these challenges they find it necessary to let go of customs of the past in order to embrace an uncertain future.

Where extended kinship obligations conflict with the demands of a modern economy, with its emphasis on individualism, there is potential for abuse of young and aging members. For example, older Maori people of traditional cultural background in New Zealand, who live on limited state pensions, often find it difficult to refuse undue pressure from younger kinsfolk for lengthy hospitality and money.[36] At the same time, older people, as guardians of tradition, can become so domineering that the initiatives of younger creative people are crushed. It is not uncommon for nuclear families and individuals belonging to extended Maori kinship systems to migrate to cities and even to foreign countries in order to avoid the traditional demands of older and younger relatives.[37]

As young people from traditional cultures seek employment in urban areas, the needs of their older kinsfolk in rural villages are increasingly neglected.[38] On the other hand,

---

[36] See Joan Metge, *The Maoris of New Zealand* (London: Routledge and Kegan Paul, 1976), 126.

[37] Paul Bergin, in his research into the migration of Maoris from New Zealand to Australia, found significant examples of this. See Paul Bergin, "New Zealand Maori Migration and Cultural Identity: The Australian Experience," doctoral thesis, Oxford University (July 1998), 345–47.

[38] See Cyril S. Belshaw, *Under the Ivi Tree: Society and Economic Growth in Rural Fiji* (London: Routledge and Kegan Paul, 1964), 160–61.

family problems may quickly arise when married children migrate for work to urban centers or even to foreign countries and take with them older members of their extended family. Often accommodations are scarce, so that older people lose any sense of privacy, but worse still is the social and linguistic isolation that can result. Older people are left to themselves during the day, and their ability to learn the language of the host countries is extremely limited. This means that they cannot communicate with outsiders and even with their grandchildren, who are quick to learn the local language and customs.

In Japan, older people were traditionally cared for by family members. However, with the declining birth rate it has become increasingly difficult to find sons or daughters to support them. For most older people the retirement allowances provided by employers and the government are scarcely enough to support them. What Harumi Befu commented in 1971 remains true today, that even when older people do live with their children, "they do not always enjoy the respected position that their parents formerly did and whatever task they perform around the house is usually menial and non-essential . . . which only helps to lower their status in the family."[39]

China: Concern for the Elderly

Confucius was insistent that while a person's parents lived, that person should not travel to distant places. In China,

---

[39] Harumi Befu, *Japan: An Anthropological Introduction* (New York: Harper and Row, 1971), 56. Male dominance in Japan is evident in corporate and political life. The older generation of men is especially traditionalist and still wields the most influence. See *The Economist* (March 29, 2014).

as more and more young people migrate to rapidly developing cities in search of work, this Confucian imperative is becoming increasingly difficult to abide by. Parents and grandparents are left behind in the countryside. There are 185 million people over sixty years of age (by 2053, this figure will jump to 487 million), and a high percentage are confined to rural areas. Because the Chinese government has become concerned that this will endanger social harmony, it has decreed that children must visit or keep in touch with their elderly parents.[40] Whether the law can be implemented remains to be seen.

Theological Reflection: Maintaining Self-Esteem in Aging

We are not really young, mature, or old in virtue of the particular determination of this or that stage of life, but in virtue of the openness with which at any stage we face, not its specific determination, but the claim within it, thus affirming and taking ourselves seriously as those who are addressed. . . . The . . . ageing are . . . called by the command of God to step out of the past into freedom. They, too, can be obedient by being youthful in this sense.

—KARL BARTH, *CHURCH DOGMATICS* III/4

---

[40] See "Rights of the Elderly: Filial Impropriety," *The Economist* (July 6, 2013).

Whatever our own culture, the challenge for aging people is to discover the art of letting go in order to embrace the future. Most Christian writers on the spiritual life grapple with the challenge of letting go by describing life as a journey or pilgrimage. Every pilgrimage calls for leaving behind whatever holds us back from deeper and deeper union with Jesus Christ, our ultimate goal. Saint Paul succinctly describes this journeying: "When I was a child, I spoke like a child, I thought like a child, I reasoned like a child; when I became an adult, I put an end to childish ways" (1 Cor 13:11). We struggle to abandon childish ways to the moment we die. The letting go is an act of wisdom, itself a gift of God.[41]

As the ailments of old age intensify, the believer can say with Saint Paul: "I want to know Christ, the power of his resurrection and the sharing of his sufferings by becoming like him in his death, if somehow I may attain the resurrection from the dead" (Phil 3:10–11). In Christ we have the ultimate source of the meaning of life. The basic foundation of our identity is Jesus Christ, and the more our prayer brings us closer to this source, the more our identity becomes that of Christ himself. The more we acquire this identity with Christ, the more our self-esteem can grow, no matter what pains and negative stereotypes we may experience as aging increases.

The writings of Saint Teresa of Avila and Saint John of the Cross are really memoirs of how they wrestled with the harsh realities of aging in the light of faith. Teresa was a person gifted with down-to-earth common sense, an engaging good humor, "a balance of piety and politics, religious

---

[41] See Peter Feldmeier, "Spirituality in Adulthood: Development and Fruition," *The Way* 43/1 (January 2004): 61.

experience and prophetic insight."[42] People of any age today could learn much from her. Threatened at times by the Inquisition and members of her own communities, she nonetheless continued with her reform of the Carmelite order and indirectly with the church itself, becoming one of the most significant persons in the post-Reformation Catholic Church.[43] Teresa was almost forty-seven—quite advanced in years for the sixteenth century—when she wrote her autobiography. It is in narrative form, a style well adapted to our postmodern times; it illustrates Teresa's engaging gifts both as listener and storyteller.[44] Writing in 1562, she looks back on her struggles to let go of attachments to worldly things around her in order to be open to the will of God. For eighteen years she had led a rather tepid religious life as a Carmelite. As long as she refused to abandon herself entirely to God, she suffered all kinds of physical and psychological pains. But in 1554 she experienced a profound conversion after reading Saint Augustine's *Confessions*, the story of his journey from his self-centeredness in adolescence and adulthood.[45] At this point she determinedly redirected her journey wholeheartedly toward Christ. In the years that followed, acting under obedience, she wrote of her experiences; *The Interior Castle* is the most reflective of her books.

---

[42] Urban T. Holmes, *A History of Christian Spirituality* (New York: Seabury Press, 1981), 99.

[43] See Gerald A. Arbuckle, *Catholic Identity or Identities? Refounding Ministries in Chaotic Times* (Collegeville, MN: Liturgical Press, 2013), 117–18.

[44] See Joseph F. Chorpenning, "Reading St. Teresa of Avila's Life Today," *Spirituality Today* 36/3 (1984): 196–209.

[45] See Cathleen Medwick, *Teresa of Avila: The Progress of the Soul* (New York: Alfred A. Knopf, 1999), 38–39.

For Teresa, those desiring to find Christ are called to become pilgrims, to journey into the very center of their soul to discover Christ's ever-loving presence. They are invited to strip themselves of useless baggage; otherwise, they will fall by the wayside with weariness. But the more they let go, the more humanly lonely they become. The loneliness can only be filled by God's abiding presence in love. Using her vivid imagination, she seeks to describe the journey of her soul and her ever-deepening relationship with God.

> [The soul] is like a castle made entirely out of a diamond or of very clear crystal, in which there are many rooms, just as in heaven there are many dwelling places. For reflecting upon it carefully . . . we realize the soul of the just person is nothing else but a paradise where the Lord says He finds His delight.[46]

The surroundings of the castle are miserably cold and dark, infested with all kinds of physical dangers. The pilgrim is invited to enter the plain-walled castle, with prayer as the key, and there discover seven dwelling places; "in each of these are many others, below and above and to the sides, with lovely gardens and fountains and labyrinths, such delightful things that you would want to be dissolved in praises of the great God who created the soul in His own image and likeness."[47] All the time, however, the soul, as it treks from dwelling to dwelling becoming closer to God

---

[46] Saint Teresa of Avila, *The Collected Works of Saint Teresa of Avila*, trans. Kieran Kavanaugh and Otilio Rodriguez, vol. 2 (Washington DC: Institute of Carmelite Studies, 1980), 283.

[47] Teresa of Avila, *The Interior Castle*, trans. Kieran Kavanaugh and Otilio Rodriguez (London: SPCK, 1979), 196.

through prayer, is tempted to turn back and leave the castle. Yet, if the soul stays on course, it experiences a spiritual transformation that is analogous to the changes of the silkworm: from birth, to the active caterpillar stage, to cocoon, and finally the butterfly stage.[48]

The fourth dwelling is the important transition stage in the journey of the soul—the stage of letting go of human attachments. This letting go is demanding and risky for the soul because the temptation to retreat to an earlier dwelling becomes intense. The soul will be afraid to let go of time-honored prayer methods, finding all kinds of intellectual reasons not to do so. But "the important thing is not to think much but to love much; and so do what which best stirs [the soul] to love."[49] Carolyn Humphreys summarizes Teresa's words at this stage by saying that if pilgrims stay on the road, "there is a change from thinking about God, to being for God. . . . This marks the beginning of the supernatural or mystical experience, because our pilgrims have moved closer to the King of Glory."[50] There is nothing narcissistic about Teresa's spirituality. She renounced the world not to escape it but rather to serve it better. At the beginning of *Way of Perfection* she grieved over the worrying problems of the world around her: the inroads of the Reformation, the growing strength of the Huguenots in France, the Inquisition, internal problems with her reforms. Her response to these challenges was clear: she and her sisters had to be powerhouses of prayer, love God and one another, and trust in Providence.[51]

---

[48] Ibid., 91–93.

[49] Ibid., 70.

[50] Carolyn Humphreys, *From Ash to Fire: An Odyssey in Prayer* (New York: New City Press, 1992), 74.

[51] Medwick, *Teresa of Avila*, 112–21.

Teresa reminds her readers that physical strength and health are not necessary for growth in the spiritual life. All that is expected of us is that we do our best: "The pastor going about zealously in his round of parish duties, and the old woman sitting in a nursing home, confused and disoriented, can both love deeply with their hearts and give what they have to give."[52]

Summary

- No unanimous definition of *young* or *old* exists. But whatever definitions are used, one thing is universally true: to move from being young to old while remaining youthful in spirit requires letting go of attachments to past times and for a process of mourning.
- In Western cultures, in which youth is an esteemed quality, older people can experience significant prejudice and discrimination. Their self-esteem is threatened. In traditional cultures, however, older people are commonly looked upon with respect, though this is changing as the values of these cultures are increasingly undermined through contact with market-oriented cultures.
- Whatever culture we belong to, and no matter our age, we are called to relinquish undue attachments to the past in order to embrace the future creatively with hope. The scriptures offer us the ways to journey through the griefs of aging: "So we do not lose heart. Even though our outer nature is wasting away, our inner nature is being renewed day by day" (2 Cor 4:16).

---

[52] Humphreys, *From Ash to Fire*, 98–99.

3

Faces of Grief

Grief's Suffocating Power

Grief makes one hour ten.
— WILLIAM SHAKESPEARE,
KING RICHARD II

Suppressed grief suffocates.
— OVID, *TRISTITIA*

They that conceal their grief find no remedy for it.
— TURKISH PROVERB

Key points covered in this chapter

- Individual or cultural grief in its many expressions is an inevitable consequence of change.
- Grief and mourning are different; the former is the sadness that follows loss, while the latter is the process of dealing with grief.
- Suppressed grief that does not lead to mourning can become so overwhelming that people and cultures feel suffocated and a sense of hopelessness grips them.

A basic assumption in this book is this: Many changes, even if people intellectually assent to them, necessitate loss, and loss evokes the sadness of grief. Not only individuals, but also cultures, experience grief. Unless this grief can be publicly articulated in mourning rituals, it will haunt the living and lead to dysfunctional behavior.[1] This chapter seeks to define grief and its many complex expressions.

Grief is something that is felt, and so it cannot be confined to a strict definition. C. S. Lewis stated in *The Problem of Pain*: "The only purpose of the book is to solve the intellectual problem raised by suffering."[2] Intellectually he was satisfied that he had personally solved questions about suffering and death, but when confronted with the reality of the death of his wife, Joy, he dramatically realized how superficial his analysis had been. Her death emotionally devastated him in ways that surprised and shocked him. Grief, he wrote, assaulted him at all levels of his being, "from day to day in all its rawness and sinful reactions and follies."[3] Even his once-secure faith was questioned. "Although *A Grief Observed* ends with faith," it nevertheless "raises all the blackest doubts *en route*."[4] Such is the overwhelming power of grief.

One early summer morning when I was walking alone along a beach in rural Ireland, it occurred to me that the sands, if they could speak, could tell many a sad tale about

[1] Marian Greenspan, *Healing Through Dark Emotions: The Wisdom of Grief* (Boston: Shambhala, 2004), 45–70; Gerald A. Arbuckle, *Change, Grief, and Renewal in the Church: A Spirituality for a New Era* (Westminster, MD: Christian Classics, 1991); and Gerald A. Arbuckle, *Humanizing Healthcare Reforms* (Philadelphia: Jessica Kingsley, 2013), 196–218.

[2] C. S. Lewis, *The Problem of Pain* (London: HarperCollins, 2002), xii.

[3] C. S. Lewis, Letter to Sister Penelope (June 5, 1951), cited in Alister McGrath, *C. S. Lewis: A Life* (London: Hodder and Stoughton, 2013), 344.

[4] Lewis, quoted in McGrath, *C. S. Lewis,* 10. See C. S. Lewis, *A Grief Observed* (London: Faber and Faber, 1961).

the trials of countless Irish people who had suffered down through centuries of oppression from foreign invaders. Later that day I recounted my thoughts to participants in a workshop that I was leading, and I invited them to comment if they wished. To my astonishment, many participants retold, often in tears, story after story of innocent family members in generation after generation who had personally suffered oppression. As I listened I began to feel not just the grief of individuals but of a culture in grief. Some participants sang haunting lyrics that movingly articulated the accumulated melancholy that comes from years of subjugation, prejudice, eviction from the land, and forced migration.

Bereavement, Grieving, Mourning

The word *bereavement* is generally used to describe the "basic fact or objective reality of loss," that is, "one can experience bereavement without an intense grief reaction."[5] *Grief* or *grieving* can be briefly described as the internal experiences of sadness, sorrow, anger, loneliness, anguish, confusion, shame, guilt, and fear, as well as various external behavior in individuals and cultures as a consequence of experiencing loss. It is possible to be bereaved without these internal and external reactions. The term *mourning*, on the other hand, refers to formal or informal rituals and internal processes of transformation that the bereaved undertakes to deal to grieving (see Chapter 4). Grieving is very much an automatic reaction to loss, but mourning requires

---

[5] Kenneth J. Doka and Terry L. Martin, *Grieving Beyond Gender: Understanding the Ways Men and Women Mourn* (New York: Routledge, 2010), 17.

a decision to relate to grief in constructive ways, that is, a willingness to acknowledge publicly that grief has occurred, to let it go, and then to be open to the world ahead.[6]

Grief Reactions

The insights of gerontologists Kenneth Doka and Terry Martin about the nature of grief are particularly helpful. Grief is "a multifaceted and individual response to loss. In short, grief is energy—an emotional reaction to loss." They emphasize that the word *emotion* is not a synonym for *feelings*; feelings are only one element of emotion. Emotions are "biologically based adaptive reactions involving changes in the physical, affective, cognitive, spiritual, behavioral systems in response to perceived environmental events of significance to the individual." I would add the words *group* or *cultures* to the word *individual,* as these also experience grief. Doka and Martin define grief as "emotion, an *instinctual* [my italics] attempt to make internal and external adjustments to an unwanted change in one's world." It involves "both inner experience and outward expression."[7] The authors elucidate the differences between physical, affective, cognitive, and spiritual reactions to grieving;[8] these reactions will manifest themselves in different behavioral ways.

Physical reactions can include a variety of somatic illnesses, for example, tiredness and exhaustion, insomnia,

---

[6] See Richard A. Kalish, *Death, Grief, and Caring Relationships* (Monterey, CA: Brooks-Cole, 1983), 218; Therese A. Rando, *Treatment of Complicated Mourning* (Champaign, IL: Research Press, 1993), 21–26.

[7] Doka and Martin, *Grieving Beyond Gender,* 37–38.

[8] See ibid., 19–25.

and fear.[9] Lewis describes his grief after the death of his wife: "No one ever told me that grief felt so like fear. I am not afraid, but the sensation is like being afraid. The same fluttering in the stomach, the same restlessness, the yawning."[10] This supports the conclusion of R. Scott Sullender that grief is "separation anxiety, an acute fear in the self over the loss or threat to lose a segment of the self associated with the lost object."[11] Grief is the cost we must pay for loving. With loss, we feel something of ourselves is destroyed.

Affective reactions of grief may be, for example, sadness, anger, shame, guilt, and a sense of powerlessness. The experience of loss—of one's youth or the power to decide things for oneself—is an inevitable and painful consequence of being human. Hamlet is agonizingly aware that he daily experiences the sadness of loss and therefore grief: "The slings and arrows of outrageous fortune . . . The heart-ache and the thousand natural shocks that flesh is heir to. . . . For who would bear the whips and scorns of time."[12] Shame can be another real reaction to loss of one's self-esteem. It is that piercing feeling of humiliation that public exposure causes,[13] and it manifests itself through behavior such as speech disruption, lowered or averted gaze, blushing, barely

---

[9] See Eunice Mortimer, *Working with the Elderly* (Aldershot: Gower, 1982), 34.

[10] Lewis, *A Grief Observed*, 7.

[11] R. Scott Sullender, *Grief and Growth: Pastoral Resources for Emotional and Spiritual Growth* (New York: Paulist Press, 1985), 28.

[12] William Shakespeare, *Hamlet*, III.i.56.

[13] See James D. Whitehead and Evelyn Whitehead, *Shadows of the Heart: A Spirituality of the Negative Emotions* (New York: Crossroad, 1995), 103; Alexander C. McFarlane and Bessel A. van der Kolk, "Trauma and Its Challenge to Society," in *Traumatic Stress: The Effects of Overwhelming Experience on Mind, Body, and Society,* ed. Bessel A. van der Kolk, Alexander C. McFarlane, and Lars Weisaeth (New York: Guilford Press, 1996), 31–32.

audible speech, or the desire to hide.[14] Shame emerges from the public uncovering of vulnerability, but guilt is something private that follows a sense of failing to maintain private and internal standards.[15] Guilt is the inner experience of having broken a moral norm; shame is the inner feeling of being looked down upon by a social group.[16] Guilt is something that can be expiated; for example, a person goes to prison for a set period following conviction for a crime. But the shame of being an ex-prisoner is impossible to erase.[17]

Spiritual reactions to loss might include a search for meaning in the midst of the loss; for example, Why did this loss have to occur to *me*? Believers in Jesus Christ may answer the question by uniting their grief with the sufferings of Christ and reaffirming their faith in his resurrection. Others may seek meaning and therefore answers in scapegoating. By passing the blame for their afflictions on to others, they conveniently distract themselves from the real causes and the efforts they must take to remove them. The chief priests were motivated in their scapegoating of Jesus by the need to find meaning behind his growing popularity. They feared they would lose their privileged social status. Rather than evaluate their own behavior, the priests prefer to make Jesus the scapegoat for their fears: "The chief priests answered [to Pilate], 'We have no king except Caesar'" (John 19:16). Self-preservation motivated

---

[14] See Thomas J. Sceff, "Shame and Conformity: The Difference-Emotion System," *American Sociological Review* 53 (1988): 395–405.

[15] See Lenore Terr, *Too Scared to Cry: Psychic Trauma in Childhood* (Grand Rapids, MI: Harper and Row, 1990), 113–14.

[16] See Gerald A. Arbuckle, *Violence, Society, and the Church: A Culture Critique* (Collegeville, MN: Liturgical Press, 2004), 79–93.

[17] See Robert Atkins, "Pauline Theology and Shame Affect," *Listening: Journal of Religion and Culture* 31/2 (1996): 140.

Loss and Shame

In New Zealand, the indigenous Maori people have, since the arrival of Europeans in the early nineteenth century, experienced almost every kind of loss except total extermination. These experiences continue to have a negative impact on their health. In a study of attitudes of senior Maori college students in 1975, I found that 73 percent agreed with the statement "Maoris have above-average gifts for manual or semi-skilled work." They had tragically accepted the dominant culture's stereotype of themselves as intellectually inferior. Teachers said that when these students of average or above average ability found their studies difficult, they would quickly lose self-confidence, saying: "What's the use! We Maoris don't have the skills anyway." In cultural terms, many Maoris felt inferior to the dominant European-originated culture. When they failed to achieve, they felt shame that they had disgraced their families and tribes. And they felt shamed as Maoris, a minority culture, in the midst of the dominant culture.

this scapegoating. As Caiaphas shrewdly observed, "It is better for one to die for the people" (John 18:14). Adolf Hitler blamed Germany's loss in the First World War on the machinations of international Jewry and the alleged failure of German Jews to be loyal citizens.[18] Ecclesiastical leaders may at times accuse some religious sisters of "disturbing the laity" with their theological comments, ignoring the fact that these sisters may be theologically and academically more skilled than themselves. To avoid confronting the real cause of their internal sadness, it is easier to scapegoat the sisters, blaming them for their own inadequacy.

---

[18] See Arbuckle, *Violence, Society, and the Church*, 136–37.

Scriptures: Grief Reactions

Sadness: The two disciples on the road to Emmaus are distressed because Jesus, their longed-for revolutionary hero, is dead: "They stood still, looking sad" (Luke 24:17).

Anger: In the Hebrew scriptures we find Jeremiah angry with God because he has lost his family and friends: "Cursed be the day I on which I was born!" (Jer 20:14).

Loneliness: "My God, my God, why have you forsaken me?" (Ps 22:1).

Hope: "And now, O Lord, what do I wait for? My hope is in you" (Ps 39:7).

There are physical signs of grief:

Weariness (Job 3:7), *breathlessness* (Job 9:18), *dry throat*: "I am weary with my crying; my throat is parched" (Ps 69:3).

Sleep disturbances (Dan 2:1), *bowel problems*, and *heart palpitations*:" My anguish, my anguish? I writhe in pain! Oh. the walls of my heart! My heart is beating wildly" (Jer 4:19).

Loss of appetite and *crying*: Hannah has lost the capacity to bear children, and so "Hannah wept and would not eat" (1 Sam 1: 7); Jesus weeps at the death of Lazarus (John 11:35).

Anxiety: Saint Paul writes: "My mind could not rest because I did not find my brother Titus there" (1 Cor 2:13).[19]

Behavioral Responses: Grief Types

We have broadly defined grief and shown that it involves multifaceted physical, psychological, and spiritual reactions. When, however, we review the many behavioral

---

[19] See Gerald A. Arbuckle, *Healthcare Ministry: Refounding the Mission in Tumultuous Times* (Collegeville, MN: Liturgical Press, 2000), 321.

responses to grief, the complexity of its reality becomes startlingly clear. I call these reactions *grief types*. At times a person, group, or culture may experience a variety of types simultaneously.

Anticipated grief is grief about some future real or possible loss. For example, people may fear that their employment will be terminated. Someone who is aging grieves over how he or she will cope with the inevitable deterioration of bodily strength or the possible loss of thinking capacity. People in the local parish fear the departure of a devoted priest or a time when the parish must amalgamate with other parishes. Just thinking about these issues evokes grief. *Intuitive grief* occurs when individuals and groups "experience and express grief in an affective way"; *instrumental grief* is grief predominantly "experienced physically, such as in a restlessness or cognition."[20] People will experience both expressions of grief, but in practice one type will tend to dominate.

Restrained grief exists when cultural norms dictate that there should be little or no visible expression of sadness over loss, as is the case in many African and Western cultures where grieving by men is far more controlled than grieving by women.[21] Sometimes a grieving person may deliberately hide the sadness and even be congratulated for doing so; people applaud the "stiff upper lip" reaction, but this leaves the bereaved feeling more and more alone. When Mrs. Gandhi's son Sanje was killed in an air crash, the television commentator remarked that she "held up well" as she traveled with his body to her home. Similar comments were made of Jacqueline Kennedy as she accompanied the

---

[20] Doka and Martin, *Grieving Beyond Gender,* 4.

[21] For example, see Jack Goody, *Death, Property, and the Ancestors: A Study of the Mortuary Customs of the Lodagaa of West Africa* (London: Tavistock Publications, 1962), 87.

body of her slain husband. The message was clear: the refusal to cry was culturally commendable. Yet the personal costs to the bereaved can be crushing.

Death of Lazarus: Restrained Grief

The reaction of Jesus to the death of Lazarus (John 10:1–44) provides an interesting example of how grief may be handled. In the culture of that time men were not expected to show deep emotion when friends and relatives died.[22] Jesus, on hearing of the death of Lazarus, followed this custom. He showed no visible signs of grieving, but seeing Mary "weeping, and the Jews who came with her also weeping, he was greatly disturbed in spirit and deeply moved" (John 10:33). So deep was his sadness that Jesus ultimately could not hold back from publicly expressing it in tears.

Chronic or *exaggerated grief* is sadness that people feel because they sense there is no way to escape their loss and its accompanying depression. Life is immobilized at the moment of loss. The bereaved give way to lasting depression: restless, apathetic, and gripped by memories.[23] Miss Havisham, the deserted bride in Charles Dickens's *Great Expectations*, experienced this morbid form of grief. She sat for years in her fading wedding gown surrounded by the ruins of her wedding reception; all the clocks of the house had been stopped at twenty minutes to nine. Geoffrey Gorer calls this behavior "mummification." A deceased person's

---

[22] See Teresa Okure, "John," in *The International Bible Commentary,* ed. William R. Farmer (Collegeville, MN: Liturgical Press, 1998), 1482.

[23] See Rando, *Treatment of Complicated Mourning,* 146–47, 177–78, 185–240, 380–81, 584.

room may be treated as a shrine in which that presence is embalmed—a life frozen at the time of loss.[24] He cites Queen Victoria, who never recovered from the death of her husband, Prince Albert. His personal possessions were kept exactly where he had left them. Here the bereaved refuses to relinquish the dead, clinging to particular objects as daily reminders that they still exist.[25] They feel guilty if they even think about letting go. The conflict between letting go and moving forward is never resolved. People who have been unemployed for a long period of time can also experience chronic grief; a sense of hopelessness grips them.

Absent grief is the failure to acknowledge any emotional reaction to significant loss. For a short period people may refuse to acknowledge loss as a way to cope, and this is healthy. But when grief does not occur for weeks or months, this can be symptomatic of a problem. However, Judy Tatelbaum adds a caution. She writes that some "deeply spiritual people accept death immediately and positively and therefore do not grieve." Or when "a long illness preceded the loved one's death, grief may have been worked through in advance."[26] *Delayed grief* occurs when people or organizations choose not to acknowledge losses on the assumption there are more important things to do! There is a superficial busyness, where often the grief is delayed until a second occasion of loss, which evokes an intense, overwhelming reaction. Suddenly repressed emotions explode, at times resulting in dysfunctional behavior.[27]

---

[24] See Geoffrey Gorer, *Death, Grief, and Mourning in Contemporary Britain* (London: Cresset, 1965), 79.

[25] See Paul Marris, *Widows and Their Families* (London: Routledge and Kegan Paul, 1958), 27.

[26] Judy Tatelbaum, *The Courage to Grieve* (New York: Harper and Row, 1980), 50.

[27] See Arbuckle, *Humanizing Healthcare Reforms*, 13–14.

Denial is "an unconscious defense mechanism whereby the truth of certain thoughts, feelings, or wishes is disavowed because of its painful or threatening nature."[28] A faulty understanding of the role of denial in the grieving process can lead to very unfortunate consequences. *Grief denial* assumes that there is no need for grieving. It is waste of time, something that strong people can ignore and get on with the job. Ecclesiastical leaders sometimes deny that parishioners should grieve over the closure of parishes; they think that closure is merely an administrative act on their part, and they are startled and annoyed when parishioners become angry. Denial, however, can at times be a positive experience, preventing people from receiving the full impact of a devastating loss and thus providing them with space to begin processing what has happened.

Grief Denial: Examples

- Denial of loss and death within healthcare cultures such as hospitals and care facilities for the aged is significant, according to psychoanalyst Wilfred Bion, due to the fact that these institutions are expected to control fundamental anxieties around life, death, and annihilation.[29] When explaining Bion's thesis, Anton Obholzer writes that in our unconscious there is a perception of health or well-being, but we have no idea of death.[30] We manage our anxieties about death

---

[28] Herbert Goldenberg, *Abnormal Psychology: A Social/Community Approach* (Monterey, CA: Brooks-Cole, 1977), 586.

[29] See Wildred Bion, *Second Thoughts* (London: Heinemann, 1967); Isabel M. Lyth, ed., *Containing Anxiety in Institutions: Selected Essays* (London: Free Association Press, 1988), 1–99.

[30] See Anton Obholzer, "Managing Social Anxieties in Public Sector Organizations," ed. Anton Obholzer and Vega Z. Roberts (London: Routledge, 1966), 170–71.

by "pushing them down" into the unconscious, and we create various institutions and rituals as defensive mechanisms. Death in Christianity is a transition to an enhanced life in Christ (1 Cor 15:54–55). In a culture of secularism, however, this appreciation of death may no longer have any meaning. Thus, the fear of death is dispelled by such institutions as hospitals and healthcare professionals. These do not give a transition to a fresh life beyond death, but in the collective unconscious they safely hold our anxieties about death.

For this reason, writes Obholzer, "our health service might more accurately be called a 'keep-death-at-bay' service." There is the prevalent illusion that healthcare services and their staffs will shelter us from death. Patients and medical personnel instinctively conspire "to protect the former from facing their fear of death and the latter from facing their fallibility."[31] The unarticulated grief and its denial, experienced especially by medical personnel become chronically embedded in healthcare cultures, leading at times to dysfunctional behavior such as bullying among staff members.[32]

- I recall an incident in the Philippines when a young Filipino priest, having attended lectures on the importance of focusing on the person of Jesus Christ in evangelization, proclaimed from the pulpit one Sunday that all the statues of the saints in the church would be removed during the coming week. One night his sleep was disturbed by cries coming from within the church. He was surprised to discover over a hundred parishioners in tears moving from statue to statue saying goodbye to their favorite saint. The priest

---

[31] Ibid., 171.
[32] See Arbuckle, *Humanizing Healthcare Reforms*, 131–60.

had denied that grief could be possible. He thought that all he had to do was to make an announcement and all would be well.

- In the early 1970s I conducted a sociological survey of a moderately sized province of a clerical religious congregation. I reported:

> In the provincial chapters over the last ten years there has been a lack of sensitivity to the manpower situation in the present and in the future. Allowing for deaths and transfers [to other provinces] the net increase in the number of priests per year for the next ten years will be approximately one. At the same time the province is aging.

The reaction to this conclusion in the culture of the province was grief denial. It was "business as usual," and ministries continued as though there would always be an ample supply of priests over the coming decade. Instead of using the personnel analysis to plan for an appropriate withdrawal from ministries over a definite time period, the province was suddenly forced in a short space of time to reduce its commitments. Local bishops and parishioners were given no warning of what was to happen. This refusal to read the "signs of the times" is an example of grief denial. The losses involved in openly planned withdrawal were too painful to acknowledge.

- An excessive exaltation of an organization's mission can be a way of denying the grief of acknowledging its failures. Administrators and employees "become hooked on the promise of the mission and choose not to look at how the system is operating." The internal chaos of an organization or ministry such as a hospital, school, and religious congregation, is dismissed "because [the institution] has a lofty mission."[33] A disproportionate focus on the inspiring language of an institution's mission statement or the founding charism of a congregation, can distract people from having to face deficiencies, injustices, or coming disasters.

Briefly, let us note other important types of grief. *Grief violence* is a dramatic type of grief. For example, people who feel their identity is threatened or has been lost may be moved to violence against their assumed oppressors. A recent study into the reasons some pious and peace-loving Muslim clerics have turned to a violent form of their faith revealed that they had lost the opportunity to obtain employment in government-controlled institutions.[34]

Migrant grief occurs when people move to unfamiliar surroundings, such as migrating to a different country, or when the elderly move out of the family home to a retirement village. It has been estimated that approximately one-third of migrants to Australia and New Zealand eventually return home, only to discover that the familiar world they had left behind no longer exists. They feel lost, with roots in no country.

Idealized grief is grief in which nostalgia for an idealized past becomes chronic. People have a utopian image of the past, failing to see its faults or inadequacies for contemporary life and to recognize that they must now move forward to embrace the future. Restorationists in the church suffer from idealized grief; they fail to acknowledge that the monarchical model of the church is today theologically

---

[33] Anne W. Schaef and Dianne Fassel, *The Addictive Organization* (San Francisco: Harper and Row, 1990), 123.

[34] See "Islamist Extremism: Green Glass Ceilings," *The Economist* (March 16, 2013), 57.

and historically irrelevant, a point strongly made by Pope Francis.[35]

Grief overload exists when individuals and cultures experience loss simultaneously from many quarters; the pressure on the bereaved becomes too much for them to manage, and they feel paralyzed.

Suppressed grief occurs when people are forced to hide their sadness over loss and public mourning is forbidden. In the early 1990s the Chinese government rounded up dissidents across the country, tightened security, and increased censorship just before the annual anniversary of the Tiananmen Square massacre for fear that people would publicly mourn the massacre and threaten the government's dictatorial authority. Since then the government continues to suppress all references to the disaster; this crusade could well be termed *forced collective grief amnesia*.[36] People who suppress the grief of others aim to destroy their hope: "Where there is no speech about grief and suffering, there can be no hope."[37] The crowd in Mark's gospel, furious that Bartimaeus, the blind beggar, was disturbing the people's orderly way of life, tried to suppress his grief, but he refused

---

[35] See Chapter 6 herein; and Antonio Spadaro, SJ, "A Big Heart Open to God," interview with Pope Francis, *America* (September 30, 2013), www.americamagazine.org/pope-interview.

[36] See Louisa Lim, *The People's Republic of Amnesia: Tiananmen Revisited* (Oxford: Oxford University Press, 2014); Ian Johnson, "The Ghosts of Tiananmen Square," *The New York Review of Books* 61/10 (2014): 31–33; "Remembering Tiananmen: The Lessons of History," *The Economist* (May 31, 2014), 25–26. In 2012 the Chinese government's campaign to repress any memory of the massacre even affected the Shanghai stock exchange. The censors tried to prevent online references to the exchange when it fell 64.89 points in a day, a number that sounds rather like June 4, 1989, the date of the massacre.

[37] Walter Brueggemann, *Hope Within History* (Atlanta: John Knox Press, 1987), 88.

to let them: "Many sternly order him to keep quiet, but he cried even more loudly" (Mark 10:48).

Catalyst grief occurs when a particular experience triggers unresolved or suppressed grief. The following examples aptly illustrate that this form of grief is particularly important for individuals and cultures.

Catalyst Grief: Examples

- The death of Princess Diana in 1997 became a catalyst for many millions of people to identify losses in their own lives that had never been resolved. At one level they mourned over the loss of a "friend" made present to them regularly through the mass media. Her death also provided the occasion for communal mourning in a culture where such ritual outlets are denied. It was reported that her death led to a steep decline in the number of people in Britain seeking help for depression. Psychiatrists claim that this unprecedented public mourning allowed people to release deeply buried emotions about some of their own personal problems. And they did it together.[38] In Diana's death, people found a focus for their free-floating grief.[39] Similarly, sometimes sicknesses or family celebrations such as Christmas can be catalysts for grieving over unacknowledged losses.
- When Pope John Paul II made his first visit to Poland in 1979 as pope, he preached at mass in Victory Square with a large cross in the background. This was the first time that the open display of a Christian symbol had been permitted in several decades by a severely

---

[38] See *Sydney Morning Herald* (December 17, 1997).
[39] See Nathan D. Mitchell, *Worship* 72/1 (1998): 44–45.

repressive government. "Let your Spirit descend and renew the face of the earth, the face of this land," the pope exhorted the people. The reaction of the congregation was spontaneous: "A cheer rose from a million throats, an enormous cathartic outpouring" of three decades of politically suppressed grief.[40]

- In Turkey in May and June 2013 a small group of environmentalists banded together in a sit-in to save an Istanbul park from being turned into a shopping mall. When Prime Minister Recep Erdogan publicly dismissed them as "marginal elements," the small protest sparked off widespread riots. Erdogan's comment became the catalyst for people in many occupations, including people from the middle class, who felt oppressed by what they perceived to be a government that progressively had failed to listen to their griefs. Erdogan's dismissive remark was the trigger that ignited their long suppressed anger.

Grieving: Stages

Authors speak of grieving as a process that may have several stages, though there is no agreement about their number or length. One writer, Granger Westberg, identifies ten stages: shock, expression of emotion, depression, physical symptoms of distress, panic, guilt, anger, immobilization, hope and affirmation of reality.[41] Colin Murray Parkes suggests these stages: numbness, yearning, disorganization,

---

[40] John Paul II, cited by Christian Caryl, *Strange Rebels: 1979 and the Birth of the Twenty-First Century* (New York: Basic Books, 2013), 201–2.

[41] See Granger E. Westberg, *Good Grief* (Philadelphia: Fortress Press, 1971).

and despair, ending with reorganization.[42] John Bowlby offers three stages: urge to recover what is lost through emotional reactions such as crying, despair, and reorganizing
life toward the future.[43] Elisabeth Kubler-Ross's model of
grieving is particularly well known: denial, anger, bargain-
ing, depression, and acceptance.[44]

The process of grieving is extremely complex, and no
one model can express this complexity; a model merely
assists us to understand in a very general way what may
happen to people or organizations in grief. People do not
automatically pass through these stages; in fact, people
can move back and forth from one stage to another, or they
may become locked in at any particular stage. Moreover, a
misunderstanding of the models of grieving may lead to the
impression that the process of sorrowing can be controlled
according to a clearly defined time period. On the contrary,
the process may take months or even years before people
become adjusted to their changed circumstances. Some
never adjust.

In all the models, however, there is general agreement
that the physical, emotional, behavioral, social, and intellectual consequences follow some predictable sequence.[45]
Despite the differences in the models of grieving, I think
four broad stages can be identified. In the first stage there is
a feeling of numbness, even denial, that loss has occurred.
In the second stage there is a mixture of strong feelings—

---

[42] See Colin Murray Parkes, "Seeking and Finding a Lost Object:
Evidence from Recent Studies of the Reaction to Bereavement," *Social
Science and Medicine* 4 (1970): 187–201.

[43] See John Bowlby, "Process of Mourning," in *The Meaning of Despair*,
ed. William Gaylin (New York: Science House, 1968), 314.

[44] Elisabeth Kubler-Ross, *On Death and Dying* (New York: Macmillan,
1969).

[45] See Thomas Attig, *How We Grieve: Relearning the World* (Oxford:
Oxford University Press, 2011), 43.

pining or nostalgia for what has been lost; restlessness; despair; anger that can be directed indiscriminately against friends, God, another cultural group, or even oneself. The third stage is noted for a feeling of drifting; the person or group searches reflectively into the past to discover what of value should be carried into the future and what should be put aside. The risk for the bereaved at this stage is to cling tenaciously to what has been lost and refuse to face the future. The fourth stage may be called the recovery or reentry period. The bereaved is able to look with some marked detachment at what has been lost; there is the recognition that life must go on and the best of the past can be carried over into the future.[46] Most writers would agree that grieving should not be considered a medical abnormality; it is medically abnormal only when it becomes pathological. Finally, grieving can be called successful when people are able to recall without severe anxiety what has been lost. Thomas Attig describes grieving as positive when people are able to relearn "the world in order to secure for those we have lost a new, vital place in ongoing and meaningful life."[47]

Examples of Cultural Trauma

Poets have sought to express the impact on cultures and people when their grieving is suppressed. It drains energy. It paralyzes people. The Roman poet Ovid (BC 43–AD 17/18) wrote in *Tristia*: "Suppressed grief suffocates." And in *In Memoriam* Alfred Tennyson wrote: "Ring out the grief that saps the mind." The overloading that is a quality of sup-

---

[46] See J. R. Averill, "Grief: Its Nature and Significance," *Psychological Bulletin* 70 (1968): 721–48.

[47] Attig, *How We Grieve*, 60.

pressed grieving smothers people's innovative skills because it is not able to be publicly expressed in mourning.

Warsaw

The German suppression of Poland was accompanied by unmatched brutality, including mass murder and the systematically planned destruction of the culture and national spirit. In 1944 the city of Warsaw was particularly targeted, with the Soviets encouraging the Nazi destruction by refusing to defend the city. Not only were close to a million inhabitants killed, but national sacred sites such as historical memorials, archives, and libraries were obliterated. The immensity of the atrocities caused cultural trauma, with devastating collective grief, that still affects Poles decades later. "The invisible mental scars are still raw. Poles find it hard to trust each other or outsiders, and many Poles feel that foreigners still lack any real understanding of Poland's wartime fate."[48]

Soviet Russia

Philosopher Jacques Derrida writes: "Nothing could be worse for the work of mourning than confusion or doubt; one has to know what is buried and where."[49] This accurately describes the scene in the Soviet Union under Stalin and the present situation under Vladimir Putin. Under

---

[48] "The Warsaw Uprising," *The Economist* (November 30, 2013), 75. See also Alexandra Richie, *Warsaw 1914: Hitler, Himmler, and the Warsaw Uprising* (London: William Collins, 2013).

[49] Jacques Derrida, cited by Alexander Etkind, *Warped Mourning: Stories of the Undead in the Land of the Unburied* (Stanford, CA: Stanford University Press, 2013), 18. See also Jacques Derrida, *Species of Marx: The State of the Debt, the Work of Mourning, and the New International*, trans. Peggy Kamuf (New York: Routledge, 1994).

Stalin millions of people were killed. They included the wretched victims of the authorities' requirement for quotas of subversives, those named in random denunciations, loyal communists, and even those who until recently had been conducting the purges. The consequence, Alexander Etkind concludes, is suppressed grieving: for lost lives, lost years, and, for many, lost ideals. Uncertainty intensifies suffering. Many loved ones just disappeared. No one knew where they were taken or whether they would return. If they were dead, which was the most likely consequence, no one knew where they were buried. In addition, people worried that they might be the next to disappear. And finally, all public efforts to express grief in mourning rituals were forbidden. Etkind notes that Germans reflect with repentance on their Nazi past, but no such reflection occurs now in Russia. Public mourning began briefly in the Khrushchev years, and in the late Soviet era, but has ceased under Putin's regime, which is choking efforts to mourn the past. Memorials are rare and are most often low-key and enigmatic.[50] Often they are constructed far from the sites of massacres to discourage memories of the past. Etkind ends his book with this relevant and poignant warning:

> Memory without memorials is vulnerable to a cyclical, recurrent process of refutations and denials. . . . Ghosts . . . refuse to leave the living until the unlawfully killed have been remembered by [Russian] culture high and low, official and popular, nationalist and cosmopolitan. Only with these multiple, infinitely numerous acts of recognizing and remembering will the new Russian culture regain its coherence and vitality.[51]

---

[50] See *The Economist* (March 16, 2013), 79–80.
[51] Etkind, *Warped Mourning*, 246.

Chile

September 11, 2013, marked the fortieth anniversary of the coup by General Augusto Pinochet that overthrew the Socialist government of Salvador Allende in Chile. The coup resulted in political repression, imprisonment, torture, disappearance, deaths, and exile of thousands of innocent people. Only a minority of those responsible have been tried. In spite of the fact that three-fifths of the population was born after the coup, a recent survey indicates that "three-quarters of Chileans believe the wounds opened in 1973 have yet to be healed."[52] Many people refused to join the country's president in a ritual of reconciliation because they feel that the cultural trauma, the result of past repression, still haunts them. They do not trust their political leaders to hear the depth of their pain. As long as this feeling continues, full national reconciliation cannot occur. There is a national impasse.

Spain

The situation in Spain illustrates how difficult it is for countries to move forward after bitter civil wars. The Spanish civil war ended in 1939, but the rival sides still defend their different versions of what happened, so that the trauma of the past still haunts the country. Two laws passed by opposing sides—the Pact of Forgetting in 1977 and the Law of Historical Memory in 2007—have done little to heal memories of grief.[53]

---

[52] "Chile's Anniversary: Divided by a Coup," *The Economist* (September 14, 2013), 46.

[53] See Jeremy Treglown, *Franco's Crypt: Spanish Culture and Memory Since 1936* (New York: Farrar, Straus, and Giroux, 2014); Jeremy Adelman,

Bougainville, Papua New Guinea:

Bougainville, an island within Papua New Guinea, was torn apart by civil war (1990–98).[54] The principal victims were thousands of innocent women and children; women were raped, tortured, and abused by all the armed forces involved in the conflict. Sixteen years later the effects of the cultural trauma, remain. What Judith Herman, an expert on collective cultural trauma, writes on the long-lasting impact of such trauma on people tragically applies to Bougainville today:

> Traumatic losses rupture the ordinary sequence of generations and defy the ordinary conventions of bereavement. The telling of the trauma story thus inevitably plunges the survivor into profound grief. Since so many of the losses are invisible or unrecognized, the customary rituals of mourning provide little consolation.[55]

Anthropologically, the corporate sapping of energy is termed *cultural trauma*. It is defined as "an invasive and overwhelming event that is believed to undermine or overwhelm one or several essential ingredients of a culture or the culture as a whole."[56] The foundational mythology of a culture, which gives it its identity, sense of meaning, and purpose, is dramatically and overwhelmingly assaulted. The

---

"Spain: Emerging from the Labyrinth," *The New York Review of Books* (June 5, 2014).

[54] See Pat Howley, *Breaking Spears and Mending Hearts: Peacemakers and Restorative Justice in Bougainville* (London: Zed Books, 2002).

[55] Judith L. Herman, *Trauma and Recovery: From Domestic Abuse to Political Terror* (London: Pandora, 2001), 188.

[56] Neil Smelser, "Psychological and Cultural Trauma," in *Cultural Trauma and Collective Identity*, ed. Jeffrey Alexander et al. (Berkeley and Los Angeles: University of California, 2004), 38.

culture is stunned, becoming, as it were, paralyzed by an event. When the Israelites in exile cried "How could we sing the Lord's song in a foreign land?" (Ps 137:4), they were still suffering cultural trauma.

Other dysfunctional symptoms of cultural trauma can be a widespread collective sense of fatalism; numbness; lethargy; chronic nostalgia for the past; persistent silencing of dissenters; scapegoating; the rise of fundamentalist movements; widespread breakdown of social and political trust; pervasive cynicism; collective loss of hope for the future; drifting without a mission and strategies; internal feuding; excessive individualism; dreams of a "messiah to get us out of the mess"; widespread bullying at all levels[57]; breakdown of trust; feelings of powerlessness; cynicism; and denial. In rigid bureaucracies it is common for groups of specialists to keep to themselves, to be overly sensitive to the importance of hierarchical status, and actively to discourage the sharing of information with other professional groups.[58] Such behavior paralyzes administrations.

No one quality points to cultural trauma; rather, several symptoms are likely to be intensely present at the same time. The term *trauma* is used because the shock is overwhelming, numbing the senses and making it difficult, if not impossible, for people and cultures to comprehend and accept what has happened.[59] The word *cultural* focuses on the cultural quality of a trauma. The shock for a culture can

---

[57] See Gerald A. Arbuckle, *Confronting the Demon: A Gospel Response to Adult Bullying* (Collegeville, MN: Liturgical Press, 2003); Arbuckle, *Humanizing Healthcare Reforms*, 131–60.

[58] See Henry Mintzberg, *Managing* (Harlow: Pearson, 2009), 169–70. I have found this behavior is detrimental to patients and is not uncommon in healthcare systems. See Arbuckle, *Humanizing Healthcare Reforms*, 185.

[59] See Dominick LaCapra, *Writing History, Writing Trauma* (Baltimore: Johns Hopkins University Press, 2001).

be sudden or it can be the result of many small events that eventually lead to overwhelming grief.

Catalysts for sudden shock can be a variety of events, for example, massive and sudden natural disasters; assassinations of leaders; mass killings; and even the less dramatic sudden and unexpected closure of ministries and parishes. In the United States the assassination of President John Kennedy left the nation in a collective trauma.[60] So did the terrorist attacks of 9/11. Many years later people can still recall the devastating effect on them of these tragic events.

I vividly recall being called by the CEO of a major Catholic hospital in Australia asking me to help her respond to the sudden decision of the government to close the hospital. As I walked into the foyer of this iconic hospital, I could feel the overwhelming sadness of the staff. People walked around stupefied by the decision, and it affected patients also.

Cultural trauma can also be the result of a cumulative series of losses over the period of time. Grief reaches overload. Such was the case with the Great Depression of the 1930s, when the mythology of capitalistic modernity was catastrophically undermined.[61]

Such also has been the case within the church, as I will shortly explain. The constant refusal by the Roman Curia to implement Vatican II, and other factors, reached a climax.

---

[60] See Ron Eyerman, "Cultural Trauma: Emotion and Narration," in *The Oxford Handbook of Cultural Sociology*, ed. Jeffrey Alexander, Ronald Jacobs, and Philip Smith (Oxford: Oxford University Press, 2012), 565.

[61] See Piotr Sctompka, "The Trauma of Social Change," in Alexander et al., *Cultural Trauma and Collective Identity*, 162. Sctompka notes that cultural trauma can even affect the biological substratum of society (161), for example, through a rise in suicide rates, the decline of the birth rate, and life expectancy (recall the case of the New Zealand Maori discussed above).

Prior to the election of Pope Francis, the church had become trapped in the debilitating effects of cultural trauma.

Theological Reflection: Overcoming Paralyzing Grief

The spirit of the Lord God is upon me . . . to comfort all who mourn . . . to give them the oil of gladness instead of mourning.

PSALM 61:1–3

With the death of Christ the disciples were traumatized. With the exception of the evangelist John, they hid in fear. Yet it is startlingly evident in the Acts of the Apostles that Jesus had left them the message that they could break through the trauma. What was the power of Christ's message and example that ultimately helped them to rise through the group trauma? What lesson does this teach us about how to work through grief, even if it is humanly overwhelming? The scriptures answer these questions.

The prophet Isaiah foretold the Messiah's coming. He is the one who is "to bring good news to the oppressed, to bind up the brokenhearted . . . to comfort all who mourn" (61:1–2). Jesus is the Messiah, the one who takes away the sins of the world (Matt 1:21), the one who "took our infirmities and bore our diseases" (Matt 8:17). He does this because through an expression of unimaginable divine pathos, he "became flesh and lived among us" (John 1:1). The divine pathos of the covenant days of the Old Testament, in which God freely suffered with the chosen people, was but a faint shadow of the way in which the Messiah was to become involved in our lives: "I am the living bread that came down from heaven . . . not like that which your ancestors ate, and they died. But the one who eats this bread will live forever" (John 6:51, 58). When Jesus enters into the human condition by becoming flesh and blood, he inevitably experiences sadness and grief. He is moved to comfort people and to challenge those who refuse to admit their own sinfulness and desperate need of him. Often he takes pity on the crowds and is moved to heal those who have lost their health, encouraging them to repent and mourn for their sins (Matt 14:4).

The reactions of Jesus to the death of Lazarus may at first sight be puzzling. Jesus uses the incident to remind Martha of the paradox that though people die, they can live if they believe in him (John 11:25–26). When he finds crowds weeping and wailing unrestrainedly around Mary and Martha, he becomes angry in the same way he did at the deathbed of Jairus's daughter (Mark 5:38–39). Why this indignation? Jesus is saddened by discovering once more the unbelief of the Jews who fail to accept the possibility that Jesus can awaken Lazarus from death. They grieve as unbelievers, those who have lost all hope. On another occasion Jerusalem is the scene of a distressing lament. Women of Jerusalem spontaneously wail over Jesus as he carries his cross to his death (Luke 23:27–31). Jesus knows that through his crucifixion he will live, but those who mourn for him are on the threshold of the destruction of Jerusalem itself. So he forbids them to lament for him and instead invites them to mourn for themselves and for their children; they and their leaders are failing to grasp the meaning of the call to repent in hope, which should be at the heart of all true gospel mourning.

Frequently Jesus confronts particular groups of people for their refusal to acknowledge their losses through mourning. One day, when pondering on the ways in which people were rejecting both John the Baptist and himself, he speaks sadly of his unsuccessful efforts to call people to let go of their false attachments to worldly ways: "We played the flute for you, and you did not dance; we wailed, and you did not weep" (Luke 7:32). He laments over "the cities in which most of his deeds of power had been done, because they would not repent" (Matt 11:20). Jesus rebukes with particular sharpness and sadness the scribes and Pharisees who do not mourn because they deny the paralysis and death of the Judaic institutions; they refuse to relinquish their irrelevant or unjust Judaic religious customs.

Jesus on one occasion gently highlights the denial of the Pharisees and the irrelevancy of the institutions. They refuse to abandon them. It is the incident of the Pharisee and the tax collector who enter the Temple to pray (Luke 18:9–14). These two people are at the opposite poles of the social scale, one at society's peak and the other a social outcast. The Pharisee speaks with speed and with many words to the Lord; it is as though he is petrified of silence lest he be forced to look behind his arrogant facade and discover his inner nothingness. The ultimate cover up on his part is to throw into his speech of self-congratulation the words: "God, I thank you that I am not like other people . . . or even like this tax collector" (Luke 18:11). The tax collector, on the other hand, with downcast eyes and the beating of his breast, grieves over his sins. And Jesus comments: "I tell you, this man went down to his home justified rather than the other; for all who exalt themselves will be humbled, but all who humble themselves will be exalted" (Luke 18:14). We can readily fall into the same trap as the Pharisee. Planning meetings and writing new mission statements to guide future action are important activities, but if we are not prepared to spend time listening to what God is saying to us in the Gospels and in prayer, then we act like the Pharisee.

As Pope Francis says in *Evangelii gaudium*: "The real new-ness is the newness which God himself mysteriously brings about and inspires, provokes, guides and accompanies in a thousand ways" (no. 12).

Saint Paul and Hope

Hope in the New Testament has three indispensable char-acteristics: anticipation, trust, and patient waiting. We *anticipate* that ultimate peace in the world to come will be ours because Jesus Christ is "our hope" (1 Tim 1:1). We *trust* the promises of Christ. But the *patient waiting* is not synonymous with passivity. On the contrary, it is a restless straining forward, not a capitulation to the status quo: "Now hope that is seen is not hope. For who hopes for what is seen? But we hope for what we do not see, we wait for it with patience" (Rom 8:24–25). And again Saint Paul says in words that have profoundly influenced Christian theology over the centuries: "Beloved, I do not consider that I have made it my own; but this one thing I do: forgetting what lies behind and straining forward to what lies ahead, I press forward on toward the goal for the prize of the heavenly call of God in Christ Jesus" (Phil 3:13–14).[62] And there is this remarkable text from Paul, writing to the Romans:

> For the creation waits with eager longing for the re-vealing of the children of God; for the creation was

---

[62] Pedro Ortiz writes that this text "has been exceptionally influen-tial in the Christian tradition as a description of the ideal of spiritual progress"; for example, Clement of Alexandria, Origen, Basil of Cae-saria, Gregory of Nyssa, Gregory the Great, and Bernard of Clairvaux frequently referred to this text. See "Philippians," in *The International Bible Commentary*, ed. William R. Farmer (Collegeville, MN: Liturgical Press, 1998), 1694.

subjected to futility, not of its own will but by the will
of the one who subjected it, in hope that the creation
itself will be set free from its bondage to decay and
will obtain the freedom of the glory of the children
of God. We know that the whole creation has been
groaning in labor pains until now; and not only the
creation, but we ourselves, who have the first fruits of
the Spirit, groan inwardly while we wait for adoption,
the redemption of our bodies. For in hope we were
saved. (Rom 8:18–24)

In this text Paul describes the poignant grieving and
mourning of all creation—humanity and the material
world—for ultimate redemption and the ability to let go
of all undue attachments to the past.[63] The implication of
these revered words is this: No person, no institution, can
remain uninvolved in the work of redemption. All persons,
young or old, and all institutions are constantly impelled
by hope to evaluate their behavior in view of the ethical
principles of love and justice and to act accordingly. This
means abandoning in faith whatever obstructs this evaluation and action.

Paul, writing to the Corinthians, returns to the same
theme and the obligation on each person and institution
to struggle to bring love and justice to all creation: "So if
anyone is in Christ, there is a new creation: everything old
has passed away; see, everything has become new! All this is
from God, who reconciled us to himself through Christ, and
has given us the ministry of reconciliation" (2 Cor 5:17–18).
We cannot stop this ministry and wait with arms folded.
Hope impels us—personally and institutionally—to let go

---

[63] Jean-Noel Aletti, "Romans," in Farmer, *The International Bible*, 1588.

whatever attachment holds us back from this ministry of reconciling the world to God.

Summary

- Grief—sadness over loss—is a complex reality characterized by physical, affective, spiritual, and behavioral reactions.
- There are many types of grief, for example, anticipated, restrained, chronic, absent, inhibited, catalyst, overload.
- Grief overload can result in cultural trauma; that is, the shock caused by dramatic change paralyzes people collectively and their culture. All kinds of dysfunctional behavior is a consequence of this paralysis.
- When Jesus entered into our human condition by becoming flesh and blood, he experienced all human griefs; by his words and actions he called us to mourn these losses in order to be open to newness beyond human imagination: "the new heavens and a new earth, where righteousness is at home" (2 Pet 3:13).

4

Grappling with Loss

From Grieving to New Life

*The public sharing of pain is one way to
let the reality sink in and let death go.*
—WALTER BRUEGGEMANN,
THE PROPHETIC IMAGINATION

Key points covered in this chapter

- A society best illustrates how it deals with loss by the way
  its members relate to the death of loved ones through
  mortuary rituals.[1]
- Mortuary rituals in traditional cultures contain a tripartite
  process: separation, liminality, and reentry.
- In Western cultures separation and liminality are given
  minimal emphasis.
- The psalms provide patterns for mourning based on the
  tripartite process in traditional cultures.

---

[1] *Mortuary* (or *morgue*) in Western countries commonly means a
physical place where a deceased person is temporarily kept before burial.
Here, however, *mortuary rituals* refers to whatever people customarily
do to bid farewell to a deceased person.

People yearn to ritualize their grief in individual and collective mourning. Following the collapse of the Twin Towers in New York in 2001, people spontaneously built shrines of flowers, candles, poems, and art in surrounding public places. Wayside crosses and flowers regularly appear on roadsides in many countries to mark the places where people were killed in motor accidents. Unspoken grief, as we explained in the last chapter, is like a powder keg waiting to be ignited into all kinds of culture/personal destroying behavior, unless it can be released in rituals of mourning.[2] This chapter describes the three tasks in the mourning process: the reorientation of the bereaved to what is lost, accompanied by a sharp sense of grief; the redefining of the bereaved identity in view of the loss; and behavioral consequences of the redefining.[3]

John Bowlby defines healthy mourning as "the successful effort of an individual to accept both that a change has occurred in the external world and that he is [thus] required to make corresponding changes in his internal, representational world and to reorganize, and perhaps to reorient, his attachment behavior accordingly."[4] Mourning rituals are shaped according to public values of particular cultures. For example, when Nelson Mandela died, there were public rituals created to accommodate the grieving needs of the international and national bereaved, but he

---

[2] See Therese A. Rando, *Treatment of Complicated Mourning* (Champaign, IL: Research Press, 1993), 146–47, 177–78, 185–240, 380–81, 584; Catherine M. Sanders, *Grief: The Mourning After: Dealing with Adult Bereavement* (New York: Wiley, 1989).

[3] See explanation in Kenneth J. Doka and Terry L. Martin, *Grieving Beyond Gender: Understanding the Ways Men and Women Mourn* (New York: Routledge, 2010), 29.

[4] John Bowlby, *Attachment and Loss*, vol. 3, *Loss* (New York: Basic Books, 1980), 18.

was finally buried according to traditionally approved tribal Thembu burial customs.[5]

A culture best reveals how it handles any significant loss by the way its members relate to the death of loved ones through mortuary rituals. The most common underlying theme in death rituals is that order, represented by life, becomes disorder with death. Cosmos is replaced by chaos. The aim of the ritual is the return of order, a process that is sometimes so lengthy that in some cultures it may take an entire generation before it is concluded. Sociologist Robert Hertz in 1907 first drew attention to a theme especially recognized in traditional cultures, namely, that the dead are in some way still among us until, by suitable rituals, they are finally separated and sent to the community of the dead, although different cultures often have conflicting ideas about the nature of this community.[6] He identified the need for two tasks in mortuary rituals: a disengagement of the individual from the collectivity, and the reallocation of the roles that the deceased once held. Rituals of the dead do not only reflect the social values of particular cultures but they also help to perpetuate these systems.[7]

Defining Mourning

Ritual, a form of storytelling, is the stylized or repetitive symbolic use of bodily movement and gesture to express

---

[5] See *The Sydney Morning Herald* (December 16, 2013).

[6] See Robert Hertz, "Contribution a une etude sur la representation collective de la mort," *Annee sociologique* 10 (1907), 48–137; and idem, *Death and the Right Hand* (New York: Free Press, 1960).

[7] See Jennifer Hockey, *Experiences of Death: An Anthropological Account* (Edinburgh: Edinburgh University Press, 1990), 29.

and articulate meaning within a cultural context.[8] The term *mourning* is usually reserved for rituals that seek to manage grief in social, visible, or conventional ways.[9] For example, wearing a particular type of clothing or constructing a memorial to what has been lost are visible rituals of mourning. So *mourning* can be defined as: "the culturally patterned expressions or rituals that accompany loss and allow others to recognize that one has become bereaved."[10]

Mourning Rituals: Types

Mourning rituals take many forms and can be categorized under these headings: personal, spontaneous, structured, and mortuary. C. S. Lewis dealt with his devastating grief following the death of his wife through a personal ritual of mourning by writing about it with powerful intensity, just as he did throughout his life when faced with losses: "Whenever you are fed up with life, start writing: ink is the great cure for all human ills, as I have found out long ago."[11] Personal rituals, such as keeping a diary or recording incidents in one's life as one approaches death, particularly reflect the needs and qualities of individuals. Examples abound of spontaneous rituals. One day when I was visiting the Vietnam Memorial in Washington DC, I noticed a veteran reverently tracing his finger over the name of a deceased colleague. On another occasion, when visiting a

---

[8] See Robert Bocock, *Ritual in Industrial Society: A Sociological Analysis of Ritualism in Modern England* (London: George Allen and Unwin, 1974), 35; Gerald A. Arbuckle, *Culture, Inculturation, and Theologians* (Collegeville, MN: Liturgical Press, 2010), 81–120.

[9] See Richard A. Kalish, *Death, Grief, and Caring Relationships* (Monterey, CA: Brooks-Cole, 1983), 218.

[10] Glennys Howarth and Oliver Leaman, eds., *Encyclopedia of Death and Dying* (London: Routledge, 2001), 127.

[11] C. S. Lewis, *The Letters of C. S. Lewis*, vol. 3, ed. Walter H. Lewis (London: Geoffrey Bles, 1966), 123.

retirement home, I observed elderly people conversationally sharing their pains with their friends while enjoying their morning cups of coffee.

Structured rituals are more formal and are expressed in preset ways. Initiation rituals, sometimes called rites of passage, are transformative rituals that celebrate important transitions of an individual or group to a new status in life, such as from work to retirement, employment to unemployment, single to married. Other examples are counseling sessions; memorials; restorative-justice processes; court trials; victim impact statements in which people describe, before the offender is sentenced, the impact of the crime on themselves; palliative care; and official government inquiries into disasters such as plane crashes. Often in palliative care the patient is encouraged to record key events in their lives. This is a healing ritual of mourning. Sometimes in-depth quality historical research allows victims to have the space to identify the causes of their grieving. For example, an excellent biography of the corrupt practices of former president Richard Nixon has provided people with the chance to name the negative impact of his behavior on innocent individuals and the nation.[12]

Examples of Structured Mourning

Global Prayer Vigil for Syria: On September 7, 2013, thousands gathered in Saint Peter's Square for a five-hour, religiously inspired, ritual of cultural mourning. It provided people present, and globally through social media, with the space to articulate their sadness over the conflict in Syria and their fears that it would escalate through the military

---

[12] See Richard Peristein, *Nixonland: The Rise of a President and the Fracturing of a Nation* (New York: Scribner, 2008).

intervention by France and the United States. Pope Francis stated: "Invoking the help of God under the maternal gaze of the Salus Populi Romani, Queen of Peace, I say: Yes, it [peace] is possible for everyone! From every corner of the world tonight, I would like to hear us cry out: Yes, it is possible for everyone!"[13]

Restorative Justice: Restorative justice focuses on the needs of victims and the offenders, as well as the community, rather than confining itself to legal principles or the punishment of the perpetrator(s). Victims become actively involved, while offenders are publicly encouraged to take responsibility through apologizing and making restitution for what has occurred. It is based on the theory of justice that believes wrongdoing is a crime against an individual or a community, rather than the state. It encourages dialogue between victim and offender and provides the highest levels of victim satisfaction and offender accountability.[14] Under the customary justice system victims remained silent onlookers to a legal process in which their personal grieving must remain unarticulated, but in restorative justice they are able to participate in a public process of mourning. No longer are they forced to mourn in private.[15]

---

[13] Pope Francis, "Homily at Peace Vigil, July 7, 2013," Vatican Radio, July 9, 2013.

[14] In New Zealand and Canada an effort was made to deal with the increasing numbers of offending indigenous youths in juvenile courts. "Such people . . . had little commitment to the legal system but might be more inclined to obey kinfolk or tribal chiefs" ("Restorative Justice: Really, Really Sorry," *The Economist* [August 2, 2003], 54).

[15] See Gerald A. Arbuckle, *Violence, Culture, and the Church: A Cultural Critique* (Collegeville, MN: Liturgical Press, 2004), 82; John Braithwaite, *Crime, Shame, and Reintegration* (Cambridge: Cambridge University Press, 1989), 152–86; Pat Howley, *Breaking Spears and Mending Hearts: Peacemakers and Restorative Justice in Bougainville* (London: Zed Books, 2002).

Public Memorials: The greater the cultural trauma, the more the mental burdens of the past haunt the living. Memorials provide people with a focus to address these burdens.[16] Almost no memorials to ordinary soldiers were established before the First World War. But so great was the trauma evoked by the deaths of thousands and thousands of soldiers in the war that memorials arose almost as a folk movement; communities in countries like Australia, New Zealand, and Britain sought to express the enormity of their grief.[17] Names of soldiers, no matter what rank, are listed on these memorials. Since 1945, Britain and most other Commonwealth countries have dedicated Remembrance Day to all those who have fallen in wars and, by extension, to denounce the horrors of all wars and the loss of trust in leaders who have allowed the mass killings to occur. The number of people who participate in these ceremonies and who visit battlefields continues to rise annually. Similarly, the cultural and individual trauma resulting from the terrorist attack on the World Trade Center in 2001 continues to affect the lives of Americans. Over twelve million people have visited the hallowed site of Ground Zero since the Memorial Plaza opened in September 2011.[18]

---

[16] Memorials can be planned to conceal the truth, thus attempting to prevent people from mourning. Such is the case with the memorial to the Nazi invasion of Hungary in 1944. It seeks to hide the fact that Hungarian officials actually collaborated with the Nazis in the deportation of 430,000 Jews to Auschwitz.

[17] See Clive Aslet, *War Memorial: The Story of One Village's Sacrifice from 1914 to 2011* (London: Penguin, 2013), 170–94.

[18] The National September 11 Memorial Museum opened on May 21, 2014, but some survivors are not ready to visit the museum because they fear it would intensify their pain: "The hesitation seems particularly acute among those who were in the city on the day of the attacks and who lost someone close" (Alan Feuer, "As 9/11 Museum Opens, These New Yorkers Will Stay Away," *The New York Times* [May 16, 2014]).

Countries have selective memories when it comes to mourning national tragedies. There are no memorials to the estimated million Britons who died in the Indian subcontinent when Britain was the world's most powerful colonial power.[19] Nor are there memorials to the millions of indigenous people who perished as a consequence of the actions of imperialist governments prior to 1945. Nor do defeated nations commonly erect memorials to their downfall. An interesting exception is a recent construction in Hamburg that calls to mind not only Holocaust victims, but the thousands killed in the Allied air raids in 1943.[20]

Consultation in the Closure of Parishes: In the Catholic Church the closure of once-flourishing parishes is a common contemporary experience. In the two examples that follow, we see how one experience intensified the grief of parishioners, but the other became a highly successful mourning ritual. In the first case the bishop decided that there were sound reasons to close a long-established parish and merge it with an adjacent parish. He asked the pastor to read the letter of closure at Sunday masses. Parishioners were stunned. Efforts to change the decision were summarily rebuffed. Years later the parishioners are still grieving the authoritarian method of closure. In the second case the bishop personally visited the parish and explained to

---

[19] See *The Economist* (November 9, 2013), 46; Astrid Erll, *Memory in Culture*, trans. Sara B. Young (London: Palgrave Macmillan, 2011), 57–61.

[20] See Colin Thubron, "Mesmerized by Germany," *The New York Review of Books* (December 19, 2013), 67. The Yasukuni Shrine, Japan, where the souls of Japan's dead, including several convicted war criminals, are enshrined also illustrates the potential divisiveness of memorials. Prime Minister Shinzo Abe visited the shrine in early 2014. China and South Korea vigorously objected because they believed the visit indicated that the Japanese government had still not mourned the fact that Japan had initiated the war.

parishioners that he wanted their advice about the future of the parish. Over several months parishioners met regularly with the local pastor, who suggested that they list reasons for and against closure. In the process the people them-selves began to recognize that there was no alternative—the parish had to merge with one close by. The process adopted by the bishop and pastor became a ritual of mourning. The process was a lengthy one, certainly, but it respected the people's rightful need to grieve and mourn.[21]

Mortuary Rituals

As already noted, the way we relate to the loss of a loved one is the primary model in our culture for other types of significant loss. Mortuary rituals are rites of passage or ini-tiation rituals in which the dead person's spirit moves into history, and the bereaved achieve new identities. In this sense mortuary rituals can be termed mortuary pilgrimages; the dead and the bereaved leave behind old identities and acquire new identities. As we will see, traditional cultures have much to teach Western societies about how to mourn losses.

Traditional Cultures

Traditional cultures are strongly group oriented, so any loss by an individual affects the entire group. Hence, the ritu-als about loss are very public and involve representatives

---

[21] Daniel Goleman offers a similar case study that analyses opposing ways of closing a Catholic school. See "Leadership That Gets Results," *Harvard Business Review on What Makes a Leader* (Boston: Harvard Business School Press, 2001), 67–68.

of the group. Rituals surrounding death guide mourners and their supporters through the pain of loss and gradually help them ease back into the life of the group. In traditional cultures mourning rituals serve social ends that are often more important than the private needs of the bereaved. Sociologist Emile Durkheim (1857–1917) writes: "Mourning is not the spontaneous expression of individual emotions. . . . It is a duty imposed by the group." It is an imposed obligation because "the foundation of mourning is the impression of a loss which the group feels when it loses one of its members."[22] Durkheim asserts that the feeling of loss weakens group membership, and public healing is therefore crucial for the unity and security of the group.[23]

Mourning: Tripartite Stages

In traditional cultures there are three clear stages in mourning rituals of the dead: separation, liminality, and reentry. In the brief first stage people are reminded that loss has occurred. The second and most critical stage is *liminality*, that is, the struggle to relinquish attachments to the deceased in order to be open to the future. For the bereaved this is the betwixt-and-between or intermediary stage between the old status with the deceased and the new status without. Their state is "frequently . . . likened to being in the womb, to invisibility, to darkness . . . to wilderness."[24] That is, in the liminal stage of the mortuary rituals there are two levels

---

[22] Emile Durkheim, *The Elementary Forms of Religious Life* (London: George Allen and Unwin, 1915), 397, 401.

[23] Anthropologist Bronislaw Malinowski, on the other hand, claims that individual emotional experience is integral to group mourning. Bronislaw Malinowski, *Magic, Science and Religion* (London: Souvenir Press, 1974), 59.

[24] See Victor Turner, *The Ritual Process: Structure and Anti-Structure* (Ithaca, NY: Cornell University Press, 1969), 169, 95.

Figure 4.1: Disengaging/Engaging for New Life

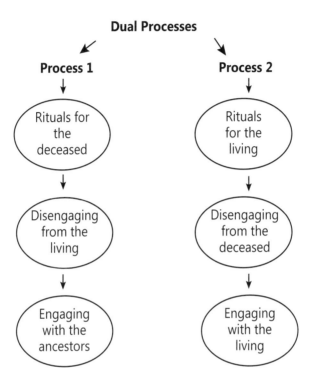

of disengagement/engagement processes operating (see Figure 4.1). First, there is a ritual process that is directed at the deceased. The dead are formally *disengaged* from the living; they are given permission, as it were, to leave this world and become *engaged* in relationships with other spirits elsewhere. They are assigned to a new, esteemed, and safe status. Among the Australian aborigines, for example, although the spirit is independent of flesh, in the sense of outlasting their disunion, a spirit is thought to haunt its former home. The liminality stage is an especially dangerous period when the departed soul is potentially vindictive and socially unrestrained; the spirit does not want the living to let it go and move into the future.[25] Thus, the spirit of the deceased must be formally encouraged to move on if it is to become an honored ancestor. The second set of disengagement/engagement rituals relates directly to the living. They must become properly *disengaged* from the negative influences of the deceased and *engage* themselves in forming a new set of social relationships or culture.[26] The liminality period for a widow in Nelson Mandela's Aba Thembu tribe in South Africa is usually a year.

Finally, at the third or *reentry* stage, rituals mark the end of mourning and the community and its members must now concentrate on living out the new set of relationships.[27] The rituals of this reentry stage must be carefully managed, because if not handled correctly they can disrupt the peaceful process of reestablishing the social order. For example, in this reentry stage for funerals of the Lodagaa people of West Africa, there are many rituals spread over several months in order to ensure that the legal and emotional roles of the deceased are firmly disassembled and redistributed among the living relatives. The most important question is the inheritance of property. If the rituals are incorrectly followed, discord results. Thus the Lodagaa "are loath to extinguish any of the dead man's relationships; hence the funeral ceremonies provide institutionalized methods for taking over of these roles by other persons. During the course of the burial service certain relationships that have been marked by satisfactory personal feelings are

---

[25] See Maurice Bloch and Jonathan Parry, eds., *Death and Regeneration of Life* (Cambridge: Cambridge University Press, 1982), 4–5.

[26] See Kenneth Maddock, *The Australian Aborigines: A Portrait of Their Society* (Harmondsworth: Penguin Books, 1974), 158–76.

[27] See Gerald A. Arbuckle, *Refounding the Church: Dissent for Leadership* (Maryknoll, NY: Orbis Books, 1993), 186–87.

provisionally re-organized, and among these are . . . friend and lover."[28]

Cultures also have norms that regulate the manner in which emotions are expressed during mourning. For example, in much of the Middle East weeping is normative and may be choreographed; women in particular may play an important role here. Among Maori people in New Zealand women may be assigned the role of leading this ritual of weeping.[29] We read in Jeremiah: "Call for the mourning women to come, send for the skilled women to come; let them quickly raise a dirge over us, so that our eyes may run with tears, and our eyelids flow with water" (Jer 9:17–18). Whether individuals actually *feel* grief is not the issue. The fact is that the community's social relations have been deeply disrupted by a death, and individuals must outwardly acknowledge it in ritually expressive ways.

Case Studies[30]

Maori Mourning Ritual

In New Zealand today the ritual for the dead among Maori remains substantially much as it has been for centuries. The fact of death is dramatically highlighted, and throughout the ritual every effort is made to express grief openly, so that at the ritual's conclusion the mourners are emotionally and physically exhausted. Maori people assume

---

[28] Jack Goody, *Death, Property, and the Ancestors: A Study of the Mortuary Customs of the Lodagaa of West Africa* (London: Tavistock Publications, 1962), 133.

[29] For other examples, see Douglas Oliver, *A Solomon Island Society: Kinship and Leadership among the Siuai of Bougainville* (Cambridge; Harvard University Press, 1955), 208–20.

[30] For other examples, see Amy Olberding, "Mourning, Memory, Identity: A Comparative Study of the Constitution of the Self in Grief," *International Philosophical Quarterly* 37/1 (1997): 29–44.

that the dead, first, must be properly put to rest; if this is not done, then the spirit of the dead person will haunt the living. Second, the bereaved must be comforted, and ties of family and social relationships must be renewed. The deep well of what it means to be Maori in today's world must also be tapped, so that all who come to the ritual may be personally and culturally refreshed. Throughout the ritual, which follows the threefold stages of separation, liminality, and reentry, rivalries are put aside. People are cooperative because all have the same purpose, namely, the need to ensure the spirit of the deceased assumes the noble role of ancestor so that it does not haunt the living, and the need for the living to readjust to the world around them and move forward.

The rites of separation begin as soon as possible after the death. Friends and relatives visit the home of the deceased, where women surrounding the body raise the *tangi* (a high-pitched, stylized wailing). Prayers are offered, and men make the first speeches of farewell to the spirit of the deceased. All the burdens of organizing the funeral are quickly taken over by the extended family to permit the immediate kin to mourn undisturbed. The body is formally laid out for viewing and is surrounded by photographs of the deceased and his or her ancestors. The immediate kinswomen of the deceased sit beside the casket and rarely leave it until the time for the burial.[31]

The liminal stage occurs over the next two to three days. The spirit of the deceased is vigorously encouraged to join its ancestors as the spokesman delivers a farewell. The process is repeated over and over again as new visitors arrive for

---

[31] See Joan Metge, *Rautahi: The Maoris of New Zealand* (London: Routledge and Kegan Paul, 1976), 261–64; Anne Salmond, *Hui: A Study of Maori Ceremonial Gatherings* (Wellington: Whitcombe and Tombs, 1977), 414–30.

mourning. "The *wairua* (spirit) of the dead, which lingers in the vicinity of the body it has so long inhabited . . . must be encouraged, by expressions of *aroha* [love] and direct commands, to go to join the ancestors."[32] At the grave members of the family symbolize the break with the deceased by throwing into the grave handfuls of dirt. This formally ends the major liminal stage whose purpose is to separate the deceased from the living and to encourage the deceased to be at peace with his or her ancestors.

The reentry of the immediate family of the deceased into the world of the living, that is, the third stage of the mortuary rituals, begins even before the actual burial ritual with tribal members discussing the future of the bereaved spouse and children. Social relationships must be reestablished. Directly after the burial a cheerful and elaborate feast is generally held for all who have attended. The bereaved family members, meanwhile, are formally taken back to their house by elders in order to conduct a rite called "trample the house." The rite aims to expel any lingering presence of the spirit of the deceased. An old woman calls out: "Welcome . . . Trample in the footsteps of the friend you have lost today!" The mourners are then welcomed to where the feast is taking place with weeping and words like: "Welcome, the bereaved. Return to your people!" The rite of reaggregation is formally completed with the unveiling of the headstone on the grave, normally a year after the burial of the deceased. The extended family pay for the stone and often decorate it themselves, sparing no effort to show the dead person that he or she is still remembered and being cared for. Prayers are said to ensure that the deceased will now finally lie in peace, satisfied with the memorial that

---

[32] Metge, *Rautahi,* 262. Metge writes that the "root meaning of *aroha* is 'love of kin', and it implies not only affectionate feelings but also the issue of those feelings in action" (66).

has been constructed in his or her honor, thus allowing the living to return finally to society without fear of being haunted by the spirit of the dead person.

Japanese Funeral Rites

Religious beliefs of the majority of Japanese are a combination of Buddhism and Shintoism, but more than 80 percent of all funerals in Japan are organized according to Buddhism. The threefold stages of mourning are clearly marked, with particular emphasis being given to the liminality stage. The separation stage (*Tsuya*, wake) begins with the washing and dressing of the body. The family and close friends spend the night beside the body reciting prayers and quietly conversing about the deceased. It is significant that the clothes worn by the deceased "are tied or done up in reverse order to the way that they would be for the living."[33] In some parts of Japan the body is dressed as a pilgrim to remind the spirit that it is now on a journey from this world to the next. Commonly the body is surrounded with incense, offerings of rice, and candles to help the deceased's spirit be at ease.

The liminality (*Soshiki*, funeral) is the hazardous stage of forty-nine days when the spirit is still attached to this world. Since this is the stage in which the spirit of the deceased can be particularly harmful to the living, great care is taken to follow the detailed rites so the spirit does not harm the living and they are able to move on with their lives in peace. The spirit is believed "to be dangerous and polluting and liable spiritually to harm or afflict those close to it in life, or even take its close kin with it to the netherworld."[34]

---

[33] Ian Reader, "Japanese Religion," in *Rites of Passage*, ed. Jean Holm and John Bowker (London: Pinter Publishers, 1994), 179.

[34] Ibid., 178.

Hence, the need for many rites that progressively aim to purify and separate the spirit from this world so that it can become an ancestor. For example, next to the body will be an offering of rice with chopsticks standing in an upright position, contrary to their normal placing for the living. The rice is for the deceased to consume on the journey to the other side; this positioning of the chopsticks reminds the departed that he or she no longer belongs to this world. Prior to the cremation a small bag containing personal things, nail clippings, and coins for the journey is prepared by the family and placed around the deceased's neck. Following the cremation the bones are placed in an urn and positioned on the family altar until the forty-ninth day. On the seventh day after the death a formal rite is celebrated and prayers are offered for the welfare of the deceased; during this rite the deceased is given a new name *(kaimyo)* to further remind the spirit that it no longer belongs to this world. During this period the closest kin, because they are especially in danger from the deceased's spirit, are themselves considered to be liminal people; as far as possible they withdraw from social relations.

The reentry stage of the ritual begins on the forty-ninth day following the death, when it is believed that the spirit of the deceased has started its new life as an ancestor. The urn is transferred to the family grave accompanied by prayers. On this day it is believed that the final judgment is passed on the deceased person's life, following which the spirit either passes to heaven or to one of the regions of hell, though it is thought that the prayers of the living can improve the lot of the departed spirit. Moreover, if the living fail to show proper respect over time for the deceased, the person's status can decline. Hence, the rituals surrounding the dead continue for many years, and annually at the three *o-bon* festivals the family meets at the grave and provides offerings for the dead.

Jewish Mourning Ritual

The Jewish mourning rituals[35] follows the tripartite process. Stage one, or the separation stage, called sitting Shiva, begins immediately following the burial; mourners return to reside as much as possible in the house of the deceased. This symbolically reminds them that death has occurred because it is there that the spirit of the deceased still lingers and also because it symbolizes "the transfer of the mantle of the deceased's role onto the shoulders of the survivor."[36] The hands of mourners must be ritually washed before they enter the Shiva house. Shoes are removed to remind mourners that they must not leave the house until the conclusion of the first phase of the liminal period of mourning. Mourners are served a meal of bread and eggs by supporters, whose task is to console them and at the same time remind them that death has occurred. The bread and eggs "are often seen in rabbinic literature as associated with the Temple or the destruction of the Temple . . . and serve as a constant reminder that rabbinic authority derives its power through the 'Bible' and the Temple, God's manifestation on earth."[37] Shiva lasts for

---

[35] See Simcha Frishbane, "Jewish Mourning Rites—A Process of Resocialization," *Anthropologica* 31/1 1989): 65–84; Howard Cooper, "Reflections on Jewish Approaches to Death, Grief, and Mourning," in *Inside Grief*, ed. Stephen Oliver (London: Society for Promoting Christian Knowledge, 2013), 98–119; Douglas J. Davies, *Death, Ritual and Belief* (London: Cassel, 1997), 127–29.

[36] Frishbane, "Jewish Mourning Rites—A Process of Resocialization," 74.

[37] Ibid., 75.

seven days, during which the mourners should not leave the house. The primary focus for the mourners is to care for themselves spiritually and to review their relationship to God in light of the death that has occurred. They do not carry out normal duties such as washing clothes, wearing makeup, or getting a haircut.

Once the week is over, the reentry stage begins; mourners are allowed to leave the house but must strictly avoid unnecessary socializing. For twenty-three days following the week's intense mourning—this thirty-day period of mourning is called Sholoshim—people slowly ease themselves back into normal living. The final period of formal mourning is Avelut, which is observed only for a parent. This period lasts for twelve months after the burial. For eleven months of that period, starting at the time of burial, the son of the deceased recites the mourner's Kaddish every day. The religious rites are generally public throughout the mourning period to remind mourners and their supporters that the former are slowly assuming new roles in society. At the end of the twelve-month mourning period, there is generally a formal unveiling ceremony, when the tombstone is revealed.

Loss in Western Societies

Mourning [in Western cultures] is treated as if it were a weakness, a self-indulgence, a reprehensible bad habit instead of a psychological necessity.
—GEOFFREY GORER,
GRIEF AND MOURNING
IN CONTEMPORARY BRITAIN

Neither the individual nor the community is strong enough to recognize the existence of death.

—PHILIPPE ARIES,
THE HOUR OF OUR DEATH

It cannot be that I ought to die. That would be too terrible.

—LEO TOLSTOY,
THE DEATH OF IVAN ILYCH

In Western societies the tripartite mourning ritual of traditional cultures has unfortunately disappeared. People are often individualistic and drift without any sense of belonging or obligations to a group. Death rituals thus are carried out with a minimum of publicity. Death (and loss) is something private, so the culture encourages all kinds of ways to ignore death or loss. Western rituals of death only very briefly acknowledge the separation stage, ignore the painful liminal stage, and move as fast as possible to the reentry stage. The cultural imperative is to let no grief be shown publicly and for the bereaved individuals, families, or organizational cultures to reintegrate into life as though nothing had happened. The whole range of grief reactions—numbness, anger, despair, guilt, the struggles to take the experience of the past into the future—are to be overlooked, repressed, or permitted only the briefest possible acknowledgment.[38] Significantly, the reading of the will that settles inheritance, generally done as soon as possible after the burial of the deceased, symbolically ends the reentry stage.

---

[38] See Rando, *Treatment of Complicated Mourning*, 6–7.

Our unwillingness to acknowledge our mortality is evident in many ways, such as attempts to hide the reality of death from the dying; hospital and funeral rituals that avoid involving the bereaved as far as possible; and the belief that at some point in time death will not be inevitable because science will have the answers. Death in traditional cultures is a community experience. However, in Western cultures it is a medical problem; death means that medical people have failed. Death, however it happens, is often cloaked in a smoke screen of euphemism, for example, "collateral damage" instead of "killing innocent people accidentally in battle situations."

We see the same dynamic at work in the occupation of the undertaker, particularly in North America, where it has become big business indeed, largely by transforming the ritual and symbolism of death to conform with the ethic of a consumer society. The contemporary funeral often has an emotional shallowness that avoids the psychological needs of sorrow and mourning. Whereas relatives once prepared the body of the deceased, this is no longer the case. People are spared the "dirtiness" of death, evident in the terminology used to soften its stark reality. For example, the "loved one," who is facially restored to "robust good health," is laid out for viewing in the "slumber" or "reposing" room. Titles such as funeral director or mortician are now substitutes for undertaker, caskets for coffins, coaches for hearses. Anything that is thought to convey morbidity or death is taboo.[39] Even grief therapy has become commercialized by the undertaking business; the bereaved are offered costly sessions on how to work through their grief. Today, most Western cultures do not demand or foster any wholesome

---

[39] See Jessica Mitford, *The American Way of Death* (New York: Simon and Schuster, 1963), 18–19.

rituals at all.[40] The way of death is a finely manipulated use of silence, denial, and avoidance of the gloomy experience that accompanies it. Death is now a logistical problem for the relevant systems analysts: clinicians, funeral directors, clergy, lawyers. It is being systematically removed from our consciousness, a form of planned obsolescence.[41]

In summary, traditional rites of passage respond to the needs of the bereaved at three levels: the psychological, the mythological, and the sociological. At the psychological level people require a ritual that culturally permits or encourages them to express fully and openly their feelings of loss. The public sharing of loss is one critically important way for the reality of loss to be accepted. People also need to see meaning in their loss, so in the ritual, cultural myths are articulated that both console and challenge the bereaved to reflect on the future. At the sociological level the bereaved need to feel that their grief is understood and shared by others, and that at the right moment they can return to society with new life and be fully accepted by it. However, commonly in Western cultures bereavement must be brief and private. The key liminal stage of mourning is to be ignored. Death is constantly depersonalized. It is portrayed as happening on the television and films or in distant countries; that is, it is something that others experience, but not us. Death is something that can be neatly controlled by turning on and off the television screen.[42] Associated with this is the mass media's fanatical concern

---

[40] See Pat Jalland, "Changing Cultures of Grief, 1850–1970," in Oliver, *Inside Grief,* 52–73.

[41] See R. W. Bailey, *The Last Enemy: A Christian Understanding of Death* (New York: Harper and Row, 1974), 1.

[42] See Gerald A. Arbuckle, *Violence, Society, and the Church* (Collegeville, MN: Liturgical Press, 2004), 104–24.

for physical health and youthfulness. This helps people to avoid having to face the inevitable reality of loss and death.

Changing Attitudes

However, there are some signs that after decades of euphemism and denial, Western societies are beginning to acknowledge loss and death once again. "Editors and art directors at Hallmark say that customers now want candour, even about terminal illness." Hallmark, which sells about half of all American sympathy cards, is preparing to produce sympathy cards to send to people who are aware that they are dying. "The word *cancer*, long shunned, now appears on mass-market cards." Other cards acknowledge the loneliness of those bereaved—"one card offers a listening ear 'after the last casserole is finished and the phone stops ringing'"—and others mention "once unspeakable events, such as suicides or miscarriages."[43]

And there are more substantial indications that attitudes are beginning to change, at least in certain areas, particularly with regard to groups of people whose grieving has been significantly suppressed or ignored. There is a growing recognition that their mourning cannot be completed until those who have committed the suppression admit the truth of what has occurred in some official manner. The pain of suffering is publicly acknowledged and the violated have the chance to articulate their pain. While individuals may have privately forgiven violators, the pain remains until the violators hear the extent of the sufferings they have inflicted and publicly apologize. Only then is it possible for the sufferers to let go the past and move forward with dignity restored. Examples will be given in the following chapter.

---

[43] "The American Way of Death," *The Economist* (June 29, 2013), 38.

Roman Ritual

Two conflicting mythologies have influenced death rituals over the centuries, especially since medieval times: one, of hope, is based on the soul's union with the paschal mystery of Christ's life, death, and resurrection; the second views death as "threatening and pessimistic . . . a summons to judgment and inevitably to punishment for sin."[44] In rituals dating from the seventh century it was the first mythology that prevailed and was reflected in a tripartite ritual. In the first stage the dying person receives communion, a symbol of the resurrection, to strengthen the soul on its journey. The passion is read, and at death the angels are exhorted to lead the soul into heavenly glory. The second stage, the liminal phase, begins with the body being accompanied by the faith community to the church, but no Eucharist is celebrated. Instead, psalms with an expressive antiphon are recited: "May the angels lead you into God's paradise, may the martyrs receive you on your arrival, and may they introduce you into the holy city of Jerusalem." The placing of the body in the church symbolically represents the liminal stage of the ritual process. The procession to the cemetery, in which the body is accompanied by members of the faith community, symbolizes the entry of the soul into the communion of saints. After medieval times, however, the second mythology of dying and death became dominant. No longer are God and the angels waiting at the end of the road to embrace the dead, but a fearful examination is to take place: "Christian death ceased to be recognized as an accomplishment of the pas-

---

[44] Richard Rutherford, *The Death of a Christian: The Rite of Funerals* (New York: Pueblo Publishing, 1980), 30.

chal exodus, and was seen instead as yet another ordeal."[45] The ritual based on the mythology of the paschal mystery became no longer dominant.

The *Order of Christian Funerals* of 1989 contains the liturgical reforms requested by Vatican II, primarily based on the first mythology, namely, the paschal mystery, but elements of the second mythology remain. The document was issued as a reference ritual and, like the *Catholic Catechism*, was not intended to be used as such, but to be translated, rearranged, and adapted to different languages and local customs. Theoretically, there is a return to the three stages characteristic of the pre-medieval liturgy, but unfortunately the first stage of separation—anointing, reception of the Eucharist as spiritual food for the journey, the foretaste of eternal life, and the vigil—is detached from the remaining two stages. At the moment of death the ritual, using traditional imagery, speaks of the soul migrating to the gates of death and paradise. But before reaching heaven it must undergo divine judgment and purification. Then the soul enters heaven accompanied by God's angels and saints. The ritual moves to the celebration of mass, which should include an appropriate homily focusing on God's compassionate love and faith in the paschal mystery as a source of comfort for mourners. Death is to be presented as the last step of an initiation that commenced at baptism. Following the mass there is space for a short eulogy to celebrate the life of the deceased. Then comes the final stage, the rite committal. For the mourners this rite with its unembellished simplicity indicates their final separation from the deceased in this life.

---

[45] Julia Upton, "Burial, Christian," in *The New Dictionary of Sacramental Worship*, ed. Peter E. Fink (Collegeville, MN: Liturgical Press, 1990), 142.

While the contemporary Catholic funeral liturgy is an effort to return to the mythology of the paschal mystery, nonetheless it has significant weaknesses:

- It still contains elements of the second medieval mythology relating to threatening judgment and the imperative to pray for the soul of the deceased, although it does not mention directly purgatory, hell, and Satan.
- It is a reference ritual, so it is not addressed to any specific culture; but conferences of bishops are expected to arrange the liturgies that relate to the cultural needs of their people; there must be a dynamic that fosters inculturation.[46] However, there are two serious obstacles to inculturation: first, Rome speaks of the need for inculturation but in fact prevents it from occurring;[47] and second, bishops commonly opt to use the reference ritual without making any changes.
- In theory the reference ritual could be used to build a three-stage ritual[48] that could incorporate appropriate lament psalms, but for reasons given in the previous comment this becomes impossible.
- The reference ritual by itself gives little emphasis to the grieving needs of mourners for two reasons: first, as the vigil is not considered essential, mourners bypass the opportunity to confront the reality of death; and second, the mass has to assume the role of the three stages in which the two processes for the mourners of disengaging from the deceased and en-

---

[46] See Gerald A. Arbuckle, *Culture, Inculturation, and Theologians: A Postmodern Critique* (Collegeville, MN: Liturgical Press, 2011), 152–88.

[47] See ibid., 175–88.

[48] See Robert Sparkes and Richard Rutherfood, "The Order of Christian Funerals: A Study in Bereavement and Lament," *Worship* 60/6 (1986): 499–510.

gaging with the future are crowded into a short time. In some places the eulogy is immediately before the mass; that is, there is a celebration of the life of the deceased that should instead be at stage three. The brevity of the unadapted ritual allows the pattern of Western cultures to "take over"; that is, mourners are encouraged to bypass stages one and two and move to the reentry stage without the space and ritual to confront their feelings of loss.

- In brief, as a model for mourning loss the unadapted reference ritual is inadequate; it mirrors the surrounding culture of denial.[49]

Theological Reflection: Psalms as Mourning Rituals

> *Consider, and call for the mourning women to come. . . . Let them quickly raise a dirge over us, so that our eyes may run down with tears.*
>
> —JEREMIAH 9:17–18

The psalms are a collection of prayers used at different times and on various occasions by the Israelites to convey thanksgiving, joy, sorrow, despair, and urgent needs. Although there are different ways to categorize them, Walter Brueggemann's division is particularly relevant to the themes of this book. Using an insight of Paul Ricoeur, he divides the psalms into three categories, *orientation, disorientation,* and *reorientation.* They fit the various stages of the community's and that individual's lifecycle.[50] The

---

[49] See Frank C. Senn, *Christian Liturgy: Catholic and Evangelical* (Minneapolis: Fortress Press, 1997), 693–705.

[50] See Paul Ricoeur, "Biblical Hermeneutics," *Semeia* 4 (1975): 1–21.

three stages that Ricoeur identified significantly resemble the ritual mourning process of *separation, liminality*, and *reentry* that so clearly characterizes the mourning rituals of traditional cultures. The psalms that fit each stage set the pattern for how we are to mourn in a faith-filled way. The psalms of *orientation*—for example, Psalms 1, 104, 8, and 37—express joy, gratitude, faith in God, and praise of the covenant. The world is described as an orderly place without tension or conflict; for example, Psalm 37 provides people with wise, practical guidelines for maintaining harmony in the world:

> Trust in the LORD, and do good;
> so you will live in the land, and enjoy se-
>   curity.
> Take delight in the LORD,
> and he will give you
> the desires of your heart. (vv. 3–4)

The psalms of *disorientation* or *dislocation* are the lament psalms that form about one-third of the psalms. Lament psalms transform the experience of liminality into an experience of approaching "God with abandonment that permits daring and visioning and even ecstasy."[51] Because the bonds of the historical relationship with the healing God remain secure, the pain of untying bonds in human relationships has a voice in lament. In form, lament models a transformation from plea to praise, from brokenness to wholeness.[52] Lament psalms are liminal prayers in which the psalmist grapples with personal loss or cultural trauma,

---

[51] Claus Westermann, trans. Douglas Scott, *Elements of Old Testament Theology* (Atlanta: John Knox Press, 1982), 103.

[52] Sparkes and Rutherford, "The Order of Christian Funerals," 507.

either clinging to what has been lost or letting it go and being open in trust to the newness that God is offering. The writers speak of chaos or cultural trauma in its many anguishing forms, for example, sickness, alienation from God or friends, exile gravely affecting their lives as individuals or the nation Israel. The former sense of order and serenity is shattered and then articulated in powerfully emotive expressions: anger, self-pity, utter loneliness, hatred. At times the manner in which the psalmist speaks to God is bluntly direct and angry, but this is possible because the psalmist knows that God is a true friend, and genuine friends understand: "My God, my God, why have you forsaken me?" (Ps 22:1). Yet, because they are friends, there is the "I-thou" relationship that God initiated with ancient Israel; the psalms call on God to be faithful to this relationship.

> O LORD, do not rebuke me in your anger,
> or discipline me in your wrath. . . .
> My soul is struck with terror, while you, you
>   O LORD—how long? . . .
> Turn, O LORD, save my life. (Ps 6:1, 3)

The psalmist angrily complains that God is not listening, because anger is accepted as a powerful human expression that must not be suppressed. Because the people are united in one covenant with God, they have every right to let their covenant partner know what they are feeling about their sufferings and how God is involved in helping to cause them. Yet deep within their hearts the people are filled with faith. Ultimately, they trust that God hears them, though there is silence: "The LORD has heard my supplication; the LORD accepts my prayer" (Ps 6:9). Psalm 74 is particularly relevant to a theme of this book, namely, that once proud Catholic culture is in chaos, in cultural trauma. The pivotal symbol of God's presence to the people, the Temple, has been destroyed, and God gets all the blame. With the devastation of the Temple, the identity of the Israelites as a people is utterly shattered:

> O God, why do you cast us off forever?
> Why does your anger smoke against the
>   sheep of your pasture? . . .
> the enemy has destroyed everything in your
>   sanctuary. (vv. 1, 3)

And there is no indication that the situation will change: "There is no longer any prophet, and there is no one among us who knows how long" (v. 9). Sheer desolation reigns supreme. The psalmist looks back to the moment of creation when God shaped the world into an orderly shape out of the primeval chaos[53]:

> You cut openings for springs. . . .
> You have fixed all the bounds of the earth;
> you made the summer and winter. (vv. 15, 17)

When the chosen people are threatened in the Exodus with destruction from the pursuing Egyptians, God by his power "divided the sea" (v. 13). Now, with the Temple's destruction, new chaos erupts. Yet Israel, encouraged by such previous

---

[53] For the biblical meaning of *chaos* see Chapter 1. *Chaos* and its many synonyms, such as "the Pit," "the grave," "wilderness," mean the state of utter confusion and fear, totally lacking in organization and predictability; chaos is the antithesis of cosmos. See Gerald A. Arbuckle, *Catholic Identity or Identities? Refounding Ministries in Chaotic Times* (Collegeville, MN: Liturgical Press, 2013), ix; Walter Brueggemann, *The Message of the Psalms* (Minneapolis: Augsburg, 1984), 70; Bernhard W. Anderson, *Creation Versus Chaos: The Reinterpretation of Mythical Symbolism in the Bible* (New York: Association Press, 1967), 132–37.

dramatic interventions, hopefully anticipates that God will restore order and identity to the nation: "Rise up, O God, plead your cause. . . . Do not forget the clamor of your foes" (vv. 22, 23). Today, many ecclesiastical congregational leaders may identify with the sentiments of this psalm. With vocations dramatically down, bishops have had to close their former large seminary buildings, and parishes are being closed or amalgamated. Because of the dramatic decline in recruits, religious congregational leaders must continue to withdraw from their once-proud symbols of identity—colleges, universities, hospitals. Many even fear that their once self-confident and successful congregations will die:

> We do not see our emblems . . .
> and there is no one among us who knows
>   how long.
> Why do you hold back your hand;
> why do you keep your hand in your bosom?
>   (vv. 9, 11)

Psalm 73 links a vivid experience of disorientation with a *glimpse* of the radical newness of the reorientation stage.[54] The psalmist is deeply disturbed and puzzled because he sees the wicked prosper: "They are not in trouble as others are; they are not plagued like other people. . . . They scoff and speak with malice; loftily they threaten oppression. . . . Therefore the people turn and praise them, and find no fault in them" (vv. 5, 8, 10). He is tempted to follow their lead: "For I was envious of the arrogant; I saw the prosperity of the wicked. . . . All in vain I have kept my heart clean and

---

[54] See John F. Craghan, *The Psalms: Prayers for Ups, Downs, and In-Betweens of Life* (Wilmington, DE: Michael Glazier, 1985), 115–67; Brueggemann, *The Message of the Psalms*, 115–27.

washed my hands in innocence" (vv. 3, 13). Then he pauses. He asks himself the question: Is there another way of look-ing at life, the way of God? He concludes that ultimately in God's good time evil will meet its own destruction.

> Truly you set them in slippery places;
> you make them fall to ruin.
> How they are destroyed in a moment. (vv.
>   18, 19)

Those who love and serve God will be rewarded. Those who cynically ignore him will be condemned: "Truly God is good to the upright. But for me it is good to be near God . . . to tell of all your works" (vv. 1, 28). This is the faith and hope that energizes the humble, trusting servant of God: "I have made the LORD God my refuge" (v. 28).

The *reorientation* psalms attest that God has unexpect-edly bestowed new gifts on individuals and on the nation. Just when the psalmists or Israel in the midst of chaos and confusion had almost given up hope of God intervening, they are suddenly through God's generous initiative show-ered with new gifts. There is now an exciting new creation, a new world of peace, unimagined energy to act in the service of God. The psalms of reorientation are as dramatic and surprising as the psalms of disorientation. In Psalm 29 we have a superb description of the transcendent power of God. The world is threatened with chaos, but it is no match for God, for nothing can resist his power, even the mighty cedars break under the force of his voice (v. 5). The mighty power of God demands celebration in song, and Psalm 29 does this poetically and precisely. Whoever recites or sings this psalm is bound to feel the confidence that God's renew-ing power gives to those who love him:

The LORD sits enthroned over the flood;
 the LORD sits enthroned as king forever.
May the LORD give strength to his people!
 May the LORD bless his people with
 peace. (vv. 10–11)

We Christians, as we look at the fading influence of our churches, missionary societies, and religious congregations, may, in the depths of our despondency, lose confidence in the power of God in Christ to renew all things. We need to be repeatedly reminded that God loves us beyond our most extravagant dreams and that God "makes Lebanon skip like a calf, and Sirion like a young wild ox" (v. 6). Out of chaos there will be a newness, but it is a newness that is a gift of God:

You have turned my mourning into dancing;
 you have taken off my sackcloth
 and clothed me with joy. (Ps 30:11)

Our task is to beg for this gift, with every fiber of our being:

To you, O LORD I call:
 my rock, do not refuse to hear me,
For if you are silent to me,
 I shall be like those who go down to the
 Pit. (Ps 28:1)

Summary

- Change commonly is "felt as catastrophic even when it is rationally recognized for the better, since it threatens the established and familiar order and requires new attitudes and behavior, changes in relationships, a move into a comparatively unknown future."[55] All loss, therefore, evokes sadness or grief. There is a deep tension in grieving: to hold on to what is valued from the past and, at the same time, to rebuild a meaningful pattern of relationships in which the loss is accepted. Mourning rituals are necessary to resolve this tension to allow people and their cultures to move forward.

- The manner in which cultures relate to death is a sure indication of the way they relate to losses in general. Mortuary rituals should be concerned with the re-socialization, whether psychological or sociological, of the individual bereaved and of the community, as well as the body and soul of the deceased. However, in Western cultures dying and death are commonly signs of institutional failure that are kept as private as possible. "Appearances are kept up; there is much small talk and forced cheerfulness while the basic feelings, the things that cry out in the heart, go unsaid."[56]

- By contrast, death rituals in traditional cultures have an overt purpose. Because death affects the well-being of all in a community, the passionate emotions of the immediate bereaved must be publicly socialized and that which is lost put to peace. The open ritual display of grief gives permission to mourners to express their sorrow rather than hiding it and thus endangering the whole group.[57]

- The lament psalms provide us with a superb faith-filled pattern for mourning losses.

---

[55] Isobel Menzies Lyth, *The Dynamics of the Social* (London: Free Association Press, 1989), 34.

[56] David Dempsey, *The Way We Die: An Investigation of Death and Dying in America Today* (New York: McGraw-Hill, 1975), 81.

[57] See Richard Huntington and Peter Metcalf, *Celebrations of Death: The Anthropology of Mortuary Ritual* (Cambridge: Cambridge University Press, 1979), 31–32.

5

Aging Institutions

Can Youthfulness Return?

And because corporate culture is so soft and complex, dysfunctional behavior is easily swept aside with subjective arguments and dismissed as not being important.

—KAI HAMMERICH AND RICHARD D. LEWIS,
FISH CAN'T SEE WATER

[Cultural trauma] is an invasive and overwhelming event that is believed to undermine or overwhelm one or several ingredients of a culture or the culture as a whole.

—NEIL SMELSER,
"PSYCHOLOGICAL AND CULTURAL TRAUMA,"

Fix your gaze on the mission, the vision, the goal that ultimately draws and inspires.

—CHRIS LOWNEY, *POPE FRANCIS*

Key points covered in this chapter

- Cultures may pass through stages: from the initial enthusiasm of founding to cultural trauma, to impasse and either refounding or extinction.
- Cultures begin the process of grief overload when mistakes inherent in the stage of their founding are not rectified and when responsible dissent is suppressed.
- Refounding necessitates that people and cultures are able to mourn their losses publicly; otherwise cultural trauma and impasse entrap them.

Cultures of a nation or of any organization have lifecycles, just as living organisms do. They learn positively to cope with the challenges of each stage, or they foster all kinds of organizational dysfunctional "diseases" that, if left unchecked, lead to the stagnation of cultural trauma, impasse, and ultimately extinction.[1] In the following model of aging cultures there are three interconnected variables for assessing the lifecycle of cultures: flexibility, controllability, and whether or not the cultures remain true to the creativity inherent in their founding story. The purpose of this chapter is to illustrate how these variables operate and influence the lifecycles of cultures.[2] We will see that creative energy declines once cultures hinder or obstruct

---

[1] See Manfred E. R. Kets de Vries and Danny Miller, *The Neurotic Organization* (San Francisco: Jossey-Bass, 1985).

[2] I define *culture* as "a pattern of meanings, encased in a network of symbols, myths, narratives and rituals, created by individuals and subdivisions, as they struggle to respond to the competitive pressures of power and limited resources in a rapidly globalizing and fragmenting world, and instructing its adherents about what is considered to be the correct way to feel, think, and behave." Gerald A. Arbuckle, *Culture, Inculturation, and Theologians: A Postmodern Critique* (Collegeville, MN: Liturgical Press, 2010), 17.

people from mourning failures to continue the innovative dynamism inherent in their founding myths.

Growing or *youthful* cultures encourage considerable flexibility because they maintain the energizing creative enthusiasm of their founding stories or myths.[3] Since they have not yet become set in their ways, there is a readiness to take on new ventures. The lessons of tradition are respected, but tradition is not the sole or primary factor influencing decision making. *Aging* cultures, however, have lost the flexibility of their founding story.[4] They have developed principles of control or powerful traditions that obstruct adaptability or creativity in the face of changing conditions. They marginalize innovators. They have become diseased. Most commonly youthful cultures become aging ones (see Figure 5.1).[5] People grow weary of having to live in an unpredictable world of experimentation and the ongoing change that this involves. They fall victim to the comforting predictability of an orderly life with its network of status—power and prestige positions. Youthful experimentation is less and less attractive to them, so all kinds of resistance mechanisms emerge that discourage or prevent change. People assume all is going well and significant improvements are not necessary or desirable; they have nothing to learn from the experience of others. This assumption of perfection, often called the utopian flaw, if left unchallenged, causes the culture to disintegrate. Extinction follows.

---

[3] *Myths* here is an anthropological term meaning "value-impregnated beliefs or stories that bind people together at the deepest level of their group life, and that they live by and for" (ibid., 30).

[4] Structures in cultures begin like frail cobwebs but quickly become prison bars unless decisions are taken to stop this process.

[5] See Tom Burns and George Stalker, "Mechanistic and Organic Systems," in *Classics of Organizational Theory*, ed. Jay N. Shafritz and Philip W. Whitbeck (Oak Park, Il: Moore, 1978), 207–11.

Figure 5.1: Organizational Cultures

	Growing/Organic Culture	Aging/Mechanistic Culture
Operative myth/mission	Growth over tradition	Tradition/status quo over growth
Vision	Clearly articulated: outward/ change oriented	Clearly articulated: inward/status-up oriented
Organizational structure	Collaborative: collaboration at top leadership levels models expectations of entire organizational culture	Rigidly hierarchical
Risk	Prepared to accept ambiguity as integral to risk-taking	Fearful of ambiguity
Structures	For growth	For status quo
Creativity	Vigorously encouraged	Vigorously discouraged: priorities given to tradition

Evaluation	Emphasis on reality testing to assess effectiveness	Reality testing not needed
Rules	Constantly checked lest they obstruct creativity	Multiplied to maintain status quo
Leaders	Not primarily administrators; concern: active, collaborative, creating, articulating a vision and strategizing for action/evaluation	Primarily administrators; priority given to detailed planning for status quo, not collaborative
Conflict resolution	Through negotiation/dialogue	Through suppression/coercion
Organizational future	Strong potential for survival/growth	Very strong potential for organizational collapse

Model Explained

A culture model aims to illuminate complex social reality by highlighting emphases and downplaying details or nuances. Nuanced explanations or details are omitted to allow us to grasp a little more clearly what is in fact a highly complex situation. Any particular culture is then compared with the model to see to what extent it resembles it or varies from it. A model is not a caricature but a construct to help us grasp complex anthropological realities.

Stage 1: Enthusiasm

Most commonly, institutions are begun by a person passionately committed to an intuition, attracting others to join in implementing this insight.[6] But there are dangers here. The founder's charismatic enthusiasm and vision are such that the immediate followers do not question the founder. The danger is that the authority structure can remain too strongly linked to one founding person and his or her vision. The second risk is that the founding person fails to clarify the mission in ways that followers feel they know and own it. The founding mythology—interrelating myths—of the group, which includes its mission, must be deeply embedded in culture. Management authority Edgar H. Schein warns: "Every organization must define and fulfil its core mission or it will not survive."[7] The third danger is the failure of the founder to establish appropriate

---

[6] See Paul Graham, "Foreword," in *Founders at Work: Stories of Start-ups' Early Days*, ed. Jessica Livingston (New York: Apress, 2008), x.

[7] Edgar H. Schein. *Organizational Culture and Leadership* (San Francisco: Jossey-Bass, 1987), 52–53, 56. John Peterman recognizes that his initially highly successful company failed because he did not formulate a precise mission statement to guide the formation of new employees. See "The Rise and Fall of the J. Peterman Company," *Harvard Business*

authority and accountability structures to guarantee the continuance of the founding mythology.

The fourth danger, when a charismatic person tries to return an existing organization to its founding enthusiasm, is that there will be people who resist change. This will intensify the grief of those who support the refounding efforts. The zoological insight of Pierre Teilhard de Chardin may well be applied to the several dangers in this first organizational stage: "Nothing is so delicate and fugitive by its very nature as a beginning."[8] In summary, "an intuition that does not find its institution is destined for a quick demise"[9] and will eventually cause much grief to a founder's followers.

Stage 2: Initial Grieving

When the dangers inherent in stage one are not addressed, the symptoms of grieving will emerge such as organizational drifting without clear goals or doubts and disagreements about the founding mythology, mission, and authority structures. A power vacuum develops. Order rather than creativity becomes the dominant emphasis. As people feel the need for stability, they create their own operative mythologies and unsuitable, rigid, and bureaucratic administrative structures. Even mythologies that existed in an organization prior to the efforts at reformation may begin to re-surface. Informed dissent and openness to innovation characteristic of stage one are smothered, and the organiza-

---

Review on What Makes a Leader (Boston: Harvard Business School Press, 2001), 135–52.

[8] Pierre Teilhard de Chardin, *The Phenomenon of Man* (New York: Harper Perennial, 2008), 120.

[9] Theophile Desbonnets, *From Intuition to Institution: The Franciscans* (Chicago: Franciscan Herald Press, 1988), 1.

tion becomes stagnant.[10] Robert Gates, US Secretary of Defense from 2006 to 2011, writes with grief that the Pentagon has lost sight of its creative founding story. It has become a rigid bureaucracy: "People at lower levels had good ideas, but they had an impossible task in breaking through the bureaucracy, being heard, and being taken seriously."[11] He describes the bureaucratic organizational disease of siloism that prevailed within the intelligence services.[12] People consequently suffered because of the lack of communication and sharing among the various departments: "Each military service was pursuing its own programs, there was no coordination in acquisition, and no one person was in charge to ensure interoperability in combat conditions. . . . All had their own agendas. It was a mess."[13]

Dissent: Explanation

Dissent is a confusing and at times a highly emotive word, especially for people who are irrevocably wedded to the status quo or who fear any form of change at all. By *dissent* I mean simply "the proposing of alternatives"; "a system that is not continuously examining alternatives is not

---

[10] Yukari I. Kane believes Apple, co-founded by the late Steve Jobs, is in decline as people seem less committed to the creativity that characterized its founding mythology. See Yukari I. Kane, *Haunted Empire: Apple After Steve Jobs* (London: William Collins, 2014). For other contemporary examples see: "Succession Planning . . . It Is Hard to Follow in the Footsteps of Greatness," *The Economist* (April 26, 2014), 52–53.

[11] Robert M. Gates, *Duty: Memoirs of a Secretary at War* (London: W. H. Allen, 2014), 133.

[12] Siloism describes the tendency of a bureaucracy to keep to itself, be overly sensitive to the importance of its hierarchical status, and discourage the sharing of information with other groups. See Gerald A. Arbuckle, *Humanizing Healthcare Reforms* (Philadelphia: Jessica Kingsley, 2013), 112.

[13] Gates, *Duty*, 129.

Restorationism in Russia

> In 1991 the Soviet Union was dissolved under the leadership of Mikhail Gorbachev, leading to the present Russian Federation. Gorbachev articulated a radically different democratic mythology from the authoritarian one that had long dominated the Soviet Union. Many were enthused by his visionary leadership. Many symbols of oppression were destroyed by his followers, including the statue of the murderous founder of the KGB, Felix Dzerzhinsky. However, Gorbachev and his successor, Boris Yeltsin, were unable to embed this mythology and appropriate political structures. The residual Soviet dictatorial mythology quickly began to resurface, gathering speed under Vladimir Putin's political leadership. A symbol of this restorationism is the recent move to bring re-erect Dzerzhinsky's statue.
>
> —Vladimir Sorokin, "Let the Past Collapse on Time,"
> *The New York Review of Books* 51/8 (2014): 4–5.

likely to evolve creatively."[14] Responsible dissent is actually a mourning ritual, because in the very act of dissenting the dissenter risks letting the past go in order to be open to the new. Open organizations encourage people who propose alternative ways of doing things because they know that organizations or cultures of all kinds age and produce deadwood.[15] New ideas and ways of doing things are seedlings out of which the future is born. However, seedlings are very fragile; they can be smothered long before they have had a chance to develop and become vigorous plants. So also with proposals for alternative ways of thinking or acting.

---

[14] John W. Gardner, *On Leadership* (New York: Free Press, 1990), 128.
[15] "I made it clear that I encouraged cultural change in the services, unorthodox thinking, and respectful dissent" (Gates, *Duty*, 134).

Dissenters threaten the well-oiled structures of an organization's process. The alternatives they propose are seen as chaotic, something to be vigorously avoided by those taking comfort in the predictable and safe ways of tradition. Distressed would-be innovators deeply committed to the founding mythology are marginalized. They threaten the status quo.[16] They begin to feel more and more powerless as opportunities to complain—that is, to mourn—are publicly denied them.

Marginalization of Dissenters: Examples

- *Xerox:* In the 1960s Xerox, a pioneer firm that developed copying machines, expanded rapidly. Senior management became concerned that it needed to supervise this speedy expansion by establishing more formal systems of accountability.[17] In its anxiety about the future Xerox recruited top management people from the auto industry; it failed to see that the orderly culture of this industry was radically different from the culture of Xerox.[18] Innovators that had made Xerox so successful in the past no longer fitted the structures and culture being imposed by auto-minded managers who would "subject any new ideas to exhaustive review [but would] kill those that did not conform to the decision-maker's analytic rules and standards [of the auto industry]."[19]

---

[16] Saint John of the Cross, for example, poignantly describes in his writings his ever-deepening grief as his efforts to challenge the Carmelite Order to refound itself were frustrated.

[17] See Erica Schoenberger, *The Cultural Crisis of the Firm* (Oxford: Blackwell, 1997), 184–86.

[18] See David Kearns and David Nadler, *Prophets in the Dark: How Xerox Reinvented Itself and Beat Back the Japanese* (New York: Harper-Business, 1992), 54, 56.

[19] Schoenberger, *The Cultural Crisis of the Firm,* 193.

The crisis in Xerox was simply the failure of its leadership to create a flexible bureaucratic structure that would continue to foster its creative founding mythology and mission. Its leaders became so anxious about the need to expand that they uncritically copied a structure of another organization totally unsuited to this vision and culture. In the process they started to kill off the intuitive energy that had made its founding so successful and unique. Innovators, feeling repressed and unheard, left the organization.

- *Kodak:* Kodak, the company that lead consumer photography for over a century, collapsed in 2012. It had become complacent, believing that the world would never accept digital cameras, yet by the early 2000s they had become inexpensive. Films were a thing of the past. But still Kodak refused to acknowledge the implications of this dramatic change in consumer needs, believing it could continue with its film products just as it had done so successfully in the past. Frustrated innovators were marginalized. Entrapped in the utopian flaw, Kodak went bankrupt.[20]

Stage 3: Grief Overload: Cultural Trauma

Malcolm Gladwell defines a tipping point as "the moment of critical mass, the threshold, the boiling point."[21] An organizational culture is at a tipping point when suppressed grief reaches overload causing cultural trauma. This will show itself in an intensification of dysfunctional behavior—the numbing impact of grief overload. People

---

[20] See Vince Barabba, *The Decision Looms: A Design for Interactive Decision-Making Organizations* (Axminister: Triarchy Press, 2011).

[21] Malcolm Gladwell, *The Tipping Point: How Little Things Can Make a Big Difference* (Boston: Little, Brown, and Company, 2000), 12.

feel that they and their culture "have been subjected to a horrendous event that leaves indelible [paralyzing] marks upon their group consciousness."[22] The culture has become innovatively stagnant, overwhelmed with paralysing sadness. Robert Gates describes the Pentagon, an organization trapped in bureaucratic denial and paralysis. It had radically lost sight of its primary mission and the passion to live it, both symptoms of cultural trauma.

> Even though the nation was waging two wars, neither of which we were winning, life at the Pentagon was largely business as usual . . . little sense of urgency, concern, or passion about a very grim situation. No senior military officers, no senior civilians came to me breathing fire about the downward slide of our military and civilian efforts in the wars. . . . The idea of speed and agility to support current combat operations was totally foreign to the building.[23]

Stage 4: Impasse: Extinction or Refounding?

Impasse is the stage when the organizational culture either totally disintegrates or enters into a refounding mode. Refounding or reforming is the process of re-owning the energy of the founding experience and creatively relating it to contemporary realities. Refounding, which goes to the root causes of cultural trauma, is not synonymous with renewal, which is confined only to relieving the symptoms of the crisis. Integral to refounding is the gift of mourning, that

---

[22] Jeffrey C. Alexander, "Toward a Theory of Cultural Trauma," in *Cultural Trauma and Collective Identity*, ed. Jeffrey Alexander et al. (Berkeley and Los Angeles: University of California, 2004), 1.

[23] Gates, *Duty*, 115.

is acknowledging the suffocating power of accumulated grief, letting it go, and moving forward. The Old Testament prophets were rituals leaders of mourning. They named the sadness and the need to let it pass in order to embrace the radically new, that is a revitalized commitment to the covenant relationship with God.[24]

Refounding Through Mourning: Examples

The following are examples of mourning rituals that individuals have initiated with the aim of breaking through the impasse created by cultural trauma. People, whose grieving has long been suppressed, are offered safe spaces to mourn and re-own founding mythologies and values dear to them.

- *Germany:* Willy Brandt, head of the German government, visited Warsaw in 1970 to see the monument for the victims of the ghetto uprising against German occupation. He spontaneously and apologetically knelt in silence for several minutes. This simple but profoundly symbolic gesture acknowledging national guilt was an act of mourning. It allowed suppressed grief to be publicly named. It "opened up a path to a triumphant rebirth of the nation."[25] As one ghetto survivor said: "He kneeled down and thereby raised his nation."[26] From Poland's perspective the apology was "effective because many other political processes in Germany

---

[24] Refounding is more fully described in Gerald A. Arbuckle, *Catholic Identity or Identities? Refounding Ministries in Chaotic Times* (Collegeville, MN: Liturgical Press, 2013), 89–142.

[25] Bernhard Giesen, "The Trauma of Perpetrators: The Holocaust as the Traumatic Reference of German National Identity," in Alexander, *Cultural Trauma and Collective Identity*, 132.

[26] Quoted in ibid., 133.

after the Holocaust had prepared the victims to hear an apology; the apology itself did not come across as a magical word."[27]

- *France:* Charles de Gaulle (1890–1970) is a refounding person of France since he was able to break through the profound despair and fatalism of France, symptoms of cultural trauma and impasse, resulting from the ignominious defeat under the Nazis in 1940. Having moved to London, where he established the Free French Forces and a government in exile, he inspired hope in a reinvigorating nationalism that ultimately led to the successful establishment in 1958 of the Fifth Republic based on a new constitution.[28]

- *South Africa: Truth and Reconciliation Commission:* Nelson Mandela accepted the challenge of forgiving the oppressors of himself and his people by establishing the Truth and Reconciliation Commission in 1995 under the chairmanship of Archbishop Desmond Tutu.[29] In his inaugural address Archbishop Tutu explained that the purpose of the commission was to provide the space for the nation to heal itself after the traumatizing experience of the apartheid years. The nation was in need of being forgiven and of forgiving. Victims of gross human rights violations were invited to give statements about their experiences; perpetrators of violence could also

---

[27] Vamik Volkan, *Killing in the Name of Identity: A Study of Bloody Conflicts* (Charlottesville: Pitchstone Publishing, 2006), 146.

[28] See Jonathan Fenby, *The General Charles de Gaulle and the France he Saved* (London: Simon and Schuster, 2010), 13–38.

[29] *Transitional justice* is the term used to describe ritual post-conflict reckoning that occurred in South Africa. In Northern Ireland in the Troubles, over two thousand of the thirty-six hundred killings are unsolved. There is no satisfactory transitional justice in place, so mourning cannot take place. This is a "septic sore" that is endangering the peace process. See "Haunted by Killers," *The Economist* (May 10, 2014), 50.

give testimony and request amnesty from both civil and criminal prosecution. The archbishop, when reflecting on the work of the commission, emphasized the importance for people to tell their story as an integral part of effective mourning. "We found that many who came to the commission attested afterwards to the fact that they had found relief, and experienced healing, just through the process of telling their story."[30]

- *Australia:* For two centuries successive governments in Australia refused to apologize for the often brutal oppression of the Aboriginal peoples. Sir William Deanne, former governor-general of Australia, wrote in 2001 that "until we achieve true and lasting reconciliation, we will remain diminished as a nation." He then insisted that the "starting point of Aboriginal reconciliation must be national acknowledgement of the past and of the effects of past injustice and oppression on the present and the future."[31] Finally, on February 13, 2008, Prime Minister Kevin Rudd, as the official national ritual leader, addressed the Federal Parliament and apologized on behalf of the nation. The apology was offered, as liturgist Gerard Moore indicates, in ritual genre and punctuated with regular repetitions of a litany: "We reflect . . . We reflect . . . We apologise . . . We apologise . . . We are sorry . . . A future where . . . A future where . . . A future based . . . A future where." Moore commented: "The apology reflected the fourfold structure of Christian wisdom. It contained 'confession' . . . and 'penance' of a sort, where the future is tied to a new collaborative approach and resolve. The sense of 'absolution' is in-

---

[30] Desmond Tutu, *No Future Without Forgiveness* (Sydney: Rider, 1999), 127.

[31] William Deane, "Reconciliation Is the Only Way Forward," *The Sydney Morning Herald* (November 9, 2001).

herent in the remarkable acceptance by the indigenous peoples, their spontaneous reaction and the deep relief felt across the nation."[32]

- *Rwanda:* The Rwandan genocide was the mass killing of Tutsi and moderate Hutu by members of the Hutu majority; approximately one million people died in four months in 1994. Every year there is a week of rituals to mourn the people killed in the horrendous event. For example, in the stadium in the capital city, Kigali, there is a dramatic portrayal of the tragedy in which six hundred and thirty performers symbolically reenact the nation's history. Their harmonious precolonial society is broken apart by European colonizers. The chronicler shouts over the top of loud throbbing music the words: "Dehumanization started!" and "We became objects!" The actors cringe and scatter in confusion. Then the killing is reenacted, and the narrator, as the sound of the music intensifies, shouts the words: "Denying human dignity, life or death became the order of the day." The actors collapse and become deathlike figures. Hundreds in the stadium do likewise in the midst of screams. Then several soldiers enter the stadium and begin to lift up the performers. Life is once more restored. The nation is made whole.[33]

- *National Commissions to Investigate Child Abuse:* In May 2009 the Irish government published a Commission's report detailing the emotional, physical and sexual abuse of thousands of children over a period

---

[32] Gerard Moore, "In Touch out of Touch: The Church and Reconciliation," in *Indigenous Australia and the Unfinished Business of Theology: Cross Cultural Engagement*, ed. Jione Havea (New York: Palgrave Macmillan, 2014), 123.

[33] See Philip Gourevitch, "Remembering in Rwanda," *The New Yorker* (April 21, 2014).

of seventy years; it drew on the testimony of almost two thousand witnesses. Early in 2013 the Australian government announced the appointment of a six-member Royal Commission to investigate institutional responses to child sexual abuse. These formal investigations are painful rituals of mourning allowing witnesses to name their abuse publicly in order to allow them to move forward.

- *Care Facilities for the Aged:* Informal rituals of mourning are common in care facilities for the aged. For example, elderly people, when they meet for coffee or at mealtime, frequently share how they feel, whether or not they have slept well, if they are hurting. Given the space to share their griefs often gives them the hope they need to get through the coming hours of pain.

Case Study: From Cultural Trauma to Refounding in New Zealand

The British Government and Maori chiefs signed a treaty in 1840 (The Treaty of Waitangi) that formally imparted to the indigenous peoples the protection, rights, and privileges of British subjects.[34] European settlers and Maori people were to have the same rights as British citizens. This is the founding myth of contemporary New Zealand. But the founding myth was increasingly ignored by the settlers to the detriment of Maori rights. For over one hundred years it remained merely a residual myth hidden away in the collective national unconscious. During this period successive New Zealand governments disregarded the rights of the Maori people, forbidding them at the same time to speak of their intensifying grief in public

---

[34] See Joan Metge, *The Maoris of New Zealand* (London: Routledge and Kegan Paul, 1976), 31.

mourning rituals; the more they remained out of sight, the better for the settlers.

Stage one, the stage of enthusiasm, began in the 1830s when Maori people first made contact with European settlers. Maoris enthusiastically adopted European economic and social customs that they considered beneficial and the settlers profited from this process. However, from 1860 through the early twentieth century the relationship between the two cultures deteriorated. An increasing number of settlers showed little patience with the mythological and structural restrictions of the treaty; if Maoris were unwilling to sell land, then it should be taken from them, with force if necessary. Thus, stage two started, initial grieving, in which the Maori people began to realize the tragedy of what was happening to them. The entire mythic structure of their culture was severely shaken, with increasingly disturbing social and political consequences. For the Maori, land was not primarily an economic unit, as the settlers considered it, but the land was where the ancestors had lived, fought on, and were buried. As they said: "Mine is the land, the land of my ancestors."[35] Their whole identity depended on this relationship to the land. Bitter warfare between the two groups erupted. The Maoris drew deeply on their traditional mythology, while at the same time mixing this mythology with Christian theology, resulting at times in fundamentalist-like movements.[36] These movements and the warfare were desperate but eventually unsuccessful efforts to mourn ritually the loss of land and identity.

At the same time, as these rituals of mourning failed, the Maoris entered the third period: grief overload: cultural trauma. Maori people fell into widespread grieving expressed in depression, apathy, disillusionment, tribal feuding, despair, and hopelessness. One Maori elder forced from his land lamented on behalf of thousands:

---

[35] A Maori axiom cited in Raymond Firth, *Economics of the New Zealand Maori* (Wellington: R. E. Owen, 1959), 368.

[36] See Gerald A. Arbuckle, *Earthing the Gospel: An Inculturation Handbook for Pastoral Workers* (Maryknoll, NY: Orbis Books, 1990), 64–73.

"Send me a handful of earth that I may weep over it."[37] Suffocated with grief, they were forbidden to mourn publicly. In 1873 Anthony Trollope reflected on what he saw: "There is scope for poetry in their past history. . . . But in regard to their future—there is hardly a place for hope."[38] By 1900 the Maori population had been reduced to forty-five thousand, and the government expected them to die out completely in a relatively short period.[39]

However, the government was mistaken. Extinction did not occur, because even by 1890 there were signs that some of the worst features of chronic grief were beginning to disappear through the initiative of highly committed and educated Maori leaders. Over decades these leaders persistently petitioned for their right to mourn publicly. This meant requesting that their language be officially recognized and nationally encouraged, that they have the right to establish public monuments to their lost heritage, and that through court action their stolen lands be returned. After lengthy resistance the government agreed in the 1980s that both parties should return to the mythology of the founding 1840 Treaty of New Zealand.[40] The Maori language is now, with English, an official national language. In 1975 the government established the Waitangi Tribunal "to deliberate and rule on alleged breaches of the Treaty of Waitangi (1840)."[41] The tribunal has become a way for Maori people not only to receive compensation for stolen lands, but also to have the chance to mourn openly. All these official changes have significantly contributed to the invigoration of indigenous morale nationally.[42]

---

[37] Cited in Firth, *Economics of the New Zealand Maori,* 370.

[38] Anthony Trollope, quoted in Keith Sinclair, *A History of New Zealand* (London: Penguin, 1959), 145.

[39] See James Belich, *Paradise Reforged: A History of New Zealand* (Auckland: Penguin Press, 2001), 191.

[40] See ibid., 466–87.

[41] Michael King, *The Penguin History of New Zealand* (Auckland: Penguin Books, 2003), 484.

[42] See ibid.; Belich, *Paradise Reforged,* 479–80.

Religious Congregations: Lifecycles

There are five interdependent elements in a vibrant culture: a founding mythology in which the vision, mission, and values are articulated; appropriate authority structures that serve the founding mythology; transformative leadership; formation of members in the founding mythology; and an openness to responsible dissent and mourning.[43] When one or more elements are lacking, the culture is in danger of falling victim to cultural trauma and impasse. The following examples illustrate what happens when congregations fail or succeed in establishing a vibrant culture.

Franciscans

Historically, many religious congregations fail to institutionalize successfully their founding mythology primarily because their founders have been unable to articulate clearly their vision and establish correct structures of government and formation of members. For example, Saint Francis of Assisi (1182–1226) founded a lay movement (though it later became clericalized) dedicated to radical corporate poverty and simplicity of life. He had few organizational skills, so his followers adapted large sections of the Dominican governmental organization as well as their apostolate to the universities.[44] But within twenty years of the death of Francis, his radical founding insight had become smothered under the weight of bureaucratic structures.[45]

---

[43] A model of a congregational lifecycle is explained in Gerald A. Arbuckle, *Out of Chaos: Refounding Religious Congregations* (New York: Paulist Press, 1988), 11–28.

[44] See Richard W. Southern, *Western Society and the Church in the Middle Ages* (Harmondsworth: Pelican, 1970), 269.

[45] See Hans Küng, *Can We Save the Catholic Church?* (London: William Collins, 2013), 337–78.

Jesuits

Saint Ignatius of Loyola (1491–1556) founded the Society of Jesus in 1540. Unlike Francis, however, he established within his lifetime governmental structures that would support his unique vision and mission of an apostolic congregation[46] and the formation processes to embed them to build a vibrant culture of the Society.[47] The mission of the Society had been clearly defined: "Finding God in all things, a spirituality that is earthbound, time conditioned, historically conscious."[48] The *Formula of the Institute* (1539) set out the basic elements of the new association that Ignatius and his companions hoped to establish, but more was required to mold recruits. For Ignatius, the *Spiritual Exercises* became "the primary means of motivating his first disciples"[49] to discern constantly what God was asking of them and the Society, but the *Exercises* would not be printed until 1548 and the *Constitutions* until 1559.[50] However, Ignatius's vicar general, Jerónimo Nadal, in particular became the highly effective traveling educator of the congregation on behalf of Ignatius and his first two successors. Nadal recognized that the recital of facts about the founding was insufficient

---

[46] Jeronimo Nadal, the vicar-general of Ignatius, commented: "The principal and most characteristic dwelling for Jesuits is not in the professed houses, but in journeyings. . . . I declare that the characteristic and most perfect house of the society is the journeys of the professed, by which they diligently seek to gain for Christ the sheep that are perishing." Cited in John O'Malley, "Travel to Any Part of the World: Jerónimo Nadal and the Jesuit Vocation," *Studies in the Spirituality of Jesuits* 1/3 (1968): 136.
[47] See John W. O'Malley, *The First Jesuits* (Cambridge, MA: Harvard University Press, 1993).
[48] Douglas Letson and Michael Higgins, *The Jesuit Mystique* (London: HarperCollins, 1995), 108.
[49] O'Malley, *The First Jesuits*, 4.
[50] Ibid., 62.

to inspire candidates. For Nadal, the use of Ignatius's *Autobiography* "became the key element in the mythmaking required to give the order its sense of location in the grander scheme of things."[51] This meant ensuring that governmental structures and formation processes based on the founding mythology had to be deeply embedded in the emerging Jesuit culture. Nadal stated in 1561 that "the Society wants men who are as accomplished as possible in every discipline that helps it in its purpose . . . and [are] not satisfied with doing it half-way!"[52] On this point O'Malley comments: "The accomplishments of the first and second generation of Jesuits confirm that advice like this was taken to heart."[53]

The administrative structures that allowed the young Society to move from an informal and charismatically led gathering of men to a formally operating organization were successfully tested when two Jesuits, Simão Rodrigues and Nicolás Bobadilla, attempted to question the authority of Ignatius as superior general.[54] This did not mean that the transfer from stage one to stage two in the lifecycle of the Society was always smooth. As Alain Woodrow writes: "Ignatius . . . left the Society a fine heritage. . . . But he had not prepared his succession." As regards the preparation for first General Congregation, following the death of Ignatius, there was "legal uncertainty and quarrels over precedence," and this "risked shattering the newly acquired unity."[55] And the screening of candidates was not always according

---

[51] Ibid., 65.

[52] Jeronimo Nadal, cited in ibid., 61.

[53] O'Malley, *The First Jesuits*, 61.

[54] See ibid., 31–32.

[55] Alain Woodrow, *The Jesuits: A Story of Power* (London: Geoffrey Chapman, 1995), 66. The seventh person to join Ignatius's founding group in 1534 was Nicholás Bobadilla, and he was to cause Ignatius and other Jesuits significant administrative problems. See Woodrow, *The Jesuits*, 40; O'Malley, *The First Jesuits*, 308.

to the set standards. Nadal, late in his life, "complained about the number in the Society who were inept, those to whom one could not confide a ministry of any substance, and the number of others in poor health or psychologically debilitated."[56] Even Ignatius himself regretted toward the end of his life that he had been at times "too easy in granting admission."[57] However, the founding mission and the governmental and ministerial mythology that had been so positively inculcated by Ignatius and his team ensured the congregation could survive and overcome these weaknesses.

Centuries later Father Pedro Arrupe was elected superior general at the Thirty-First General Congregation shortly before the closing of Vatican II. During that gathering Arrupe told the delegates what he would require for the refounding of the institute. Jesuits must face a world that demanded gospel responses to "atheism, Marxism, ecumenism, problems of social and international justice"; Jesuits must be pioneers in fostering the interaction between the gospel and cultures throughout the world, using, where possible, whatever assistance the human sciences could provide. He did not minimize the dramatic nature of the cultural shift that this would require of Jesuits: "Adaptation must bear on the structures, works, men, and mentalities. This operation is not easy!"[58] Arrupe recognized that over the centuries the Society had drifted away from the founding story of Ignatius, with its focus on the most urgent needs of the times. It had fallen victim to the utopian flaw and too wedded to the status quo in its ministries, losing the art of discernment so fundamental to the vision of Ignatius and drifting without

---

[56] Nadal, cited in O'Malley, *The First Jesuits*, 61.

[57] Ibid., 58.

[58] Pedro Arrupe, *One Jesuit's Spiritual Journey: Autobiographical Conversations with Jean-Claude Dietsch* (Anand Gujarat Sahitya Prakash, 1986), 26.

reference to the founding mission of Ignatius, sure signs of emerging cultural trauma.

Arrupe challenged the Society to reclaim its founding experience and to apply it creatively to contemporary realities. This meant, as an essential requirement, that the *Spiritual Exercises* must again be given a central role in the Society.[59] Through his insistence on the *Exercises,* Arrupe, following the example of Ignatius, called individual Jesuits and the Society to enter into the heart of the paschal mystery in order to abandon the irrelevant, personally and ministerially, so as to be open to the new. In this he was fulfilling the task of a ritual leader of mourning in the Society.

Pedro Arrupe moved rapidly in an inspirational manner to challenge Jesuits to implement the General Congregation's decrees. In a letter to all Jesuits he articulated the obstacles to refounding and the need for a

> pedagogy to avoid the danger of falling into extremes of unrealizable utopian radicalism or pusillanimous fear which presents those as impossible for us. . . . The implementation of the decrees . . . demands of us before everything else a deep and clear affirmation of faith . . . a change of attitudes, of criteria, of ways of thinking, and of the standard and style of life.[60]

Arrupe exercised leadership in a "hands-on, value-driven" manner in two ways: through letters on key issues of renewal and refounding, and by visitations to Jesuit provinces either personally or through his assistants. There

---

[59] See Michael Campbell-Johnston, "Being and Doing," *The Tablet* (August 4, 1992).

[60] Pedro Arrupe, cited in Thomas P. Faase, *Making the Jesuits More Modern* (Washington DC: University of America Press, 1981), 338, 337. Faase analyses the impact of Vatican II on Jesuit culture.

were letters on obedience and service (1967); on poverty, witnessing, solidarity, and austerity (1968); on discernment (1971); and on the four priorities of refounding of Jesuit life (1971).[61] In late 1974 the Thirty-second General Congregation opened. Its central document was on faith and justice. The delegates clarified the implications of this document for the spiritual life, lifestyles, apostolates, and formation of Jesuits.[62] As a follow-up to the Congregation, Arrupe wrote letters titled "Genuine Integration of the Spiritual Life and the Apostolate" (1976), "Apostolic Availability" (1977), and "Inculturation" (1978). He was equally prolific in communications explicitly on the Jesuit charism and its relationship to the contemporary apostolate.

As happened in the time of Saint Ignatius, Father Arrupe's authority was severely questioned by small Jesuit groups,[63] but he did not waver in his commitment to refounding. He had an extraordinary grasp of the contemporary secular challenges to the gospel, a deep personal feeling of oneness with the mission of Saint Ignatius, the gift of seeing the practical implications of these insights for Jesuits, and a remarkable gift of being able to inspire people to follow his leadership. The secret of his refounding strength is to be found in his spiritual ability—in the face of deep personal suffering, often intensified by significant opposition to his refounding movement from within the Society and eventually from Rome itself—to face death with notable equanimity and hope. Writing before his retirement and his sickness, he said significantly: "In reality,

---

[61] See Arrupe, *One Jesuit's Spiritual Journey*, 27.

[62] See Faase, *Making the Jesuits More Modern*, 45–82.

[63] See Paul Vallely, *Pope Francis: Untying the Knot* (London: Bloomsbury, 2013), 54–55. Pope Francis refers to this situation in Antonio Spadaro, SJ, "A Big Heart Open to God," interview, *America* (September 30, 2013), www.americamagazine.org/pope-interview.

death . . . is for me one of the most anticipated events."[64] A key characteristic of a truly refounding person is his or her ability to identify with the Gethsemane experience of Jesus Christ. This Arrupe willingly accepted.

Marists

The Society of Mary (Marist Fathers) was founded as an apostolic religious congregation by a priest, Jean-Claude Colin, in Lyons, France, and formally approved in 1836.[65] The mission of Western Oceania, South Pacific, was entrusted to the Society by Pope Gregory XVI in the same year. Zealous recruits joined the Society, and many departed for the difficult and often dangerous mission fields of Oceania. However, serious internal problems inherent in the founding stage of the congregation haunted it for many years. Colin was unable to lead the young Society of Mary in its lifecycle journey from stage one to stage two for a variety of interconnected reasons.

Colin was a charismatic, saintly person and a highly effective spiritual director of his men in their zeal for personal ascetical holiness; they were devoted to him. Here lies the paradox. While he successfully fostered in his men an intense, faith-filled ascetical commitment to Jesus Christ, he hesitated to articulate clearly for the young congregation a *specific* founding mythology that would allow it to define its apostolic uniqueness, including a focused mission, and an integrated spirituality.[66] Unfortunately, he kept to himself key inspiring elements of an apostolic founding

---

[64] Arrupe, *One Jesuit's Spiritual Journey*, 103.

[65] The problems of founding raised in this case study may be common to some other congregations formed in the nineteenth century.

[66] See Jan Snijders, *A Mission Too Far . . . Pacific Commitment* (Adelaide: ATF Theology, 2012), 381–82.

mythology that were only discovered by historians after Vatican II. These included that Mary, Mother of Mercy, is coming to the aid of a world that in the Enlightenment had drifted from its traditional Christian roots; and that Mary calls Marists to labor with her to bridge the gap between modernity and the church.[67] This meant that the Society has found it difficult to develop an identity with a sharply defined apostolic mission that could sustain it through the inevitable difficulties of institutional and geographical growth.

In addition to his hesitancy to clarify a distinctive founding mythology and the mission of the young Society, Colin was unable to develop appropriate structures of government and management.[68] Nor did he delegate their development to another Marist. As Marist historian Father Jan Snijders notes: "Colin's bent to remain non-involved in anything but spiritual direction, became a negative asset when he was called upon to direct the Pacific missions."[69] Contrary to sound advice, he assigned bishops in remote Oceania to be both the episcopal *and* the religious superiors of Marists. Consequently the episcopal authority dominated until after Vatican II, and dedicated Marists were effectively pressured in practice to become diocesan clergy.[70] This problem was not resolved until the late 1960s.

The founder was also very reluctant to write a definitive set of constitutions. From 1836 to 1872 the Society lacked any officially approved constitutions that would have specified its mission, spirituality, and governmental structures.

---

[67] See Jan Snijders, *The Age of Mary* (Rome: Maristica, 1988), 20–71.

[68] As the Society expanded, the provinces tended to develop their own distinctive operative mythologies based on their different national cultures, theologies, and particular ministries.

[69] Snijders, *A Mission Too Far . . . Pacific Commitment*, 385.

[70] Ibid., 67–68.

Without these constitutions it was difficult to develop appropriate formation processes. Moreover, at Rome's insistence, the approved constitutions of 1872 incorporated the monastic/ascetical model of religious life. This was contrary to the apostolic emphasis that the founder desired. The monastic/ascetical emphasis is evident, for example, in the 1873 General Chapter, which decreed that the *primary* task of provincial chapters is to promote religious discipline according to the monastic rules as set out in the constitutions and to inquire into the financial administration of houses. No mention was made of the need to foster apostolic creativity in ministry. The 1893 provincial chapter of one province directed that Marists, including pastors, were "prohibited from going out after the evening meal for unnecessary visits." The assumption was that a Marist house is a quasi-monastery. Such factors meant that the congregation was left drifting and in increasing grief because it lacked a clearly articulated corporate, apostolic mission.

Grief turned to cultural trauma when the congregation faced the challenge of adjusting to the directives of Vatican II. When Marists assembled at the General Chapter for renewal (1969–70), the inherent weaknesses in their existing congregational culture and governmental structures became increasingly obvious. The Society decentralized administratively. The delegates, lacking a clearly expressed congregational founding mythology and mission to shape new administrative structures, decided it would be advisable to decentralize simply for pragmatic reasons. Because "a certain attitude or mentality of mistrust of all central authority"[71] existed in the provinces, the central administration was left paralyzed. For example, it was discouraged

---

[71] Roger Durmortier, Superior General, *Report to the XXIVth General Chapter: The Facts and Problems* (Rome: Padri Maristi, 1977), para. 234.

from making canonical visitations of provinces because no one quite knew the purpose of such visitations. Some time later the general administration tentatively tried to react to major problems surfacing in the provinces, but, uncertain about its authority, it found it difficult to anticipate crises and to lead the provinces to face the pastoral and spiritual implications of the General Chapter of 1969–1970.

The unresolved weaknesses in the stage one lifecycle of the Society's founding continue to bedevil it; the impasse with its accompanying grief endures.[72] Successive General Chapters have been unable to develop an acceptable global mission because the Society has lacked a unique apostolic founding mythology. Consequently, the last General Chapter of 2009 did not attempt to formulate a specific mission statement. At the chapter's conclusion, it was decided to re-adopt, without further clarification, the vague mission statement of the chapter of 2001, despite the fact that between 2001 and 2009 conditions within and outside the Society had changed significantly.

The challenge now is not so much refounding the Society but rather, guided by the Spirit and Mary, Mother of Mercy, of solidly founding it for the first time on the inspiring Colinian mythology as discovered in historical research of recent decades and with appropriate governmental structures. The sage Marian insights of the founder are as relevant today as they were in his time and are in line with the compassionate pastoral exhortations of Pope Francis. Colin advised his men to avoid condemning the way people act, but rather "to offer them a helping hand, [to] go along with what is needed and not to be too demanding. . . . I take

---

[72] See Snijders, *A Mission Too Far . . . Pacific Commitment*, which for Marist readers is a ritual of mourning; as they read it, Marists are able to identify the source of contemporary governance and ministerial weaknesses and what now needs to be done to make appropriate corrections.

a broad [pastoral] path; I wait till their faith grows. . . . Yes, we must begin a new church." Colin often reminded Marists that they are to act in a "hidden and unknown" way.[73] By this he meant that Marists by their behavior are to promote a church that shuns clericalism, triumphalism, and involvement in authoritarian political and social structures—in contrast to the pre-revolutionary church in France. Marists cannot do this alone: "The apostles needed [Mary] to guide them, and to be in a sense the foundress of the church." Now "she will make her presence felt even more than in the beginning."[74]

Theological Reflection: Journeying Through Impasse

> *Our impasses do not yield to hard,*
> *generous work, to the logical solutions*
> *of the past.*
>
> —CONSTANCE FITZGERALD, OCD,
> "IMPASSE AND DARK NIGHT"

Cultural traumas result in institutional impasse. Institutions and their members reach, as it were, a stalemate, with no hope of the future because the darkness surrounding them is so great. This is why the spirituality of Saint John of the Cross is relevant; he invites us to find a way through personal and cultural traumas and impasses. He views life as a pilgrimage in which the pilgrim begins to feel joy in God's presence and in prayer. Then suddenly the soul is cast

---

[73] Jean-Claude Colin, *A Founder Speaks: Jean-Claude Colin* (Rome: Marist Fathers, 1975), 40, 350.

[74] Ibid., 336.

into a darkness in which there is no pleasure to be found in God or the world. The soul is at an impasse. No merely human effort, says Saint John, no matter how logically prepared it may be, can break this impasse.

Spirituality, Trauma, and Impasse

The dedicated person will be confronted with two impasses or periods of darkness in which he or she is called by God first to the purification of the senses and then of the spirit. Speaking of the first phase of darkness, the purification of the senses, Saint John writes: "This small gate is the dark night of sense, in which the soul is despoiled and denuded . . . that it may be capable of walking along the narrow road which is the night of the spirit."[75] These bleak transitional periods, in which the soul is called to forsake attachments that hold it back from receiving the transforming presence of God's love, are called by Saint John the dark nights of the soul. These periods are stages of mourning in which people are invited to transcend themselves and to reach out in hope, all the time struggling to put aside the "self sufficiency which comes from the prompting and the limitations of our ego."[76] They are times of intense loneliness. People are at an impasse. Normal human solutions to problems of this nature no longer work. Yet the experiences have the potential to be catalysts for unimagined new life. The constant danger, however, is that people will reject these

---

[75] John of the Cross, "The Dark Night," in *The Collected Works of Saint John of the Cross,* trans. Kieran Kavanaugh and Otilio Rodriguez (Washington DC: ICS Publications, 1979), 320.

[76] Peter Slattery, *The Springs of Carmel* (Sydney: St Paul Publications, 1990), 88.

opportunities for new life, taking refuge instead in despair and cynicism.[77]

Symbols: Dark and Night

John uses robustly descriptive symbols to describe the journey of the soul and in particular the periods of transition: *dark* and *night.* Both words have rich biblical roots. Dark symbolizes all that is painful to the pilgrim, such as suffering, sin, and selfishness. Thus "a deep and terrifying darkness descended upon [Abram]" as God revealed to him the future poverty and enslavement of his descendants (Gen 15:22–13); and following the crucifixion of Jesus, "darkness came over the whole land" (Luke 23:44). *Night,* however, emphasizes the mysterious actions of God in the midst of the darkness within and around us. We read that Jacob wrestled with God in the night until daybreak (Gen 32:24); the psalmist speaks of God's actions: "If you try my heart, you will visit me by night" (Ps 17:3); and Jesus "spent the night in prayer to God" (Luke 6:6:12) and began his agony in the night (John 13:30). For Saint John the night is the place of encounter:

> O night that has united
> The Lover with His beloved
> Transforming the beloved in her Lover.[78]

Finally, the word *soul* for John simply means that "the whole human person [is] being acted upon by God, stressing the

---

[77] See Constance Fitzgerald, "Impasse and Dark Night," in *Living with Apocalypse: Spiritual Resources for Social Compassion,* ed. Tilden H. Edwards (San Francisco: Harper and Row, 1984), 94.

[78] John of the Cross, "The Dark Night," 296.

interior dimensions of our personhood."[79] The dark night of the senses is the renunciation of all things we value. This is not only the abandonment of sin, but the abandonment of everything that restrains the soul from flying like a bird to God. John's darkness involved the horrible experience of being kidnapped and imprisoned at the age of thirty-nine by members of his own congregation because they feared his calls for their radical reform.[80] Thirteen years later he was falsely charged by them for libel.

Saint John describes what happens to the soul in the second period of purification, the dark night of the spirit:

> God divests the faculties, affections and senses, both spiritual and sensory, interior and exterior. He leaves the intellect in darkness, the will in aridity, the memory in emptiness and the affections in supreme affliction, bitterness and anguish.[81]

John then depicts what happened to him after the purification of the spirit: the empty space was filled by divine love.[82]

The dark night of the spirit, which is more excruciating than the dark night of the senses, is noted for its particularly agonizing experience of loneliness, alienation, and isolation, in which the participant finds it very difficult to pray and fulfill everyday tasks.[83] In this darkness, where faith alone supports us, we cry out to God for help as we

---

[79] Francis K. Nemerck and Marie T. Coombs, *The Spiritual Journey: Critical Thresholds and Stages of Adult Spiritual Genesis* (Collegeville, MN: Liturgical Press, 1987), 104. This book is highly recommended.

[80] See Richard P. Hardy, *The Life of Saint John of the Cross* (London: Darton, Longman, and Todd, 1987), 61–98.

[81] John of the Cross, "The Dark Night," 333.

[82] See ibid., 334–35.

[83] Ibid., 335.

struggle to abandon every attachment that holds us back from continuing our pilgrim vocation.

Yet there is consolation. Saint John writes:

> It should be known that if a person is seeking God, his Beloved is seeking him much more . . . God is the principal agent in this matter, and that He acts as the blind man's guide who must lead it by the hand to the place it does not know how to reach (to supernatural things of which neither its intellect, nor will, nor memory can know the nature).[84]

As in all rituals of mourning, the person must say yes to the experience. There is a point of choice: flee back to a familiar past, be paralyzed by the chaos, or move forward in hope by letting go attachments to what has gone before. To attempt to escape back to the past, or to be held captive by the chaos, only leads to increased frustration.[85] It is the gift of hope that will keep the soul focused and striving to be open to the loving presence of God. "Hope," writes John, "empties and withdraws the memory from all creature possessions . . . and fixes it on that for which it hopes."[86] Only hope can release the soul from its attachments to the past.

Contemporary Relevance

John understood the darkness could be caused by a wide range of trauma-evoking problems, for example, financial difficulties, loneliness, marginalization by friends, conflicts

---

[84] John of the Cross, "The Living Flame of Love," in Kavanaugh and Rodriguez, *The Collected Works of Saint John of the Cross*, 620–21.

[85] See John of the Cross, "The Ascent of Mount Carmel," in Kavanaugh and Rodriguez, *The Collected Works of Saint John of the Cross*, 70.

[86] John of the Cross, "The Dark Night," 381.

within community. Father Iain Matthew, OCD, an authority on Saint John's writings, when reflecting on the nature of John's darkness, says that "we can add our own reversals to the list: unnecessary changes in what we held dear; repression where one had come to enjoy new freedom; the company of people who mock or side-line one's convictions; . . . the great reversals of bereavement, illness, ageing and dying."[87] Matthew concludes that it is correct to widen the scope when we wish to plumb the depths of the meaning of this darkness for ourselves and the world at large. He quotes Saint John Paul II, reflecting on Saint John's life: "Physical, moral and spiritual suffering, like sickness—like the plagues of hunger, like war, injustice, solitude, the lack of meaning in life, the very fragility of human existence, the sorrowful knowledge of sin, the seeming absence of God—are for the believer all purifying experiences which might be called night of faith."[88] We could add to this the present chaotic state of the church,[89] a point to be explained in the following chapter; the pain of seeing thousands of innocent people being killed by warfare; the corruption of political and industrial power; the bullying that occurs in all walks of life; and the feeling of being confronted by an impasse that renders one humanly powerless.

Summary

- Aging in organizations means a decreased capacity to face up to problems: "The same problems an organi-

---

[87] Iain Matthew, *The Impact of God: Soundings from Saint John of the Cross* (London: Hodder and Stoughton, 1995), 81.

[88] John Paul II, Apostolic Letter for the Fourth Centenary of the Death of Saint John of the Cross, "Master in the Faith," no. 14 (December 1990), www.ewtn.com/library/papaldoc/jpmaster.htm.

[89] See Fitzgerald, "Impasse and Dark Night," 93–116.

zation has been dealing with for years begin to seem increasingly insurmountable as an organization ages." This aging is not inevitable, provided an organization is prepared to rejuvenate itself continuously.[90]

- Grief begins to grip an organization whenever it fails to deal with its unresolved problems. They become ghosts that increasingly haunt it and ultimately threaten its very existence. Organizational cultures begin the process of grief overload when mistakes inherent in stage one of their founding are not rectified, for example, the failure to clarify their mission and to establish appropriate structures and formation programs to ensure that the founding mythology is deeply embedded and continues to energize people. An institution without a clearly defined mission lacks focus, and resources inevitably become dissipated.[91]

- People and cultures, when trapped in the overwhelming grief of cultural trauma, must have the space to mourn publicly; mourning can begin only when official leadership acknowledges the trauma and apologizes for what has happened.

- Religious congregations can experience cultural trauma; failure to mourn the grief of this trauma results in dramatic loss of energy and innovation, leading eventually to extinction.

- The spirituality of Saint John of the Cross, with its emphasis on overcoming through faith and hope the terrifying experience of personal and group darkness, is especially relevant in times of cultural trauma.

---

[90] Ichak Adizes, *Corporate Lifecycles: How and Why Corporations Grow and Die and What to Do About Them* (Englewood Cliffs, NJ: Prentice-Hall, 1988), 4.

[91] See W. Jack Duncan et al., *Strategic Management of Health Care Organizations* (Oxford: Basil Blackwell, 1995), 176–90.

6

The "Francis Factor"

Re-owning the Vatican II Story

On the sociological level . . . [the church] . . . exhibits organisational traits which in many respects resemble those of secular organisations.

—MADY A. THUNG,
THE PRECARIOUS ORGANISATION

No large institution will overnight transform its paradigm into something entirely different . . . especially not an institution so deeply embedded in human culture as the Roman Catholic Church.

—JOHN W. O'MALLEY, SJ,
"DEVELOPMENTS, REFORMS,
AND TWO GREAT REFORMATIONS"

The church is scandalously badly run. Francis will have only a short time to make urgently needed changes.

—THE ECONOMIST, MARCH 16, 2013

Key points covered in this chapter

- The mythology of the pre-conciliar church was noted for its authoritarian, centralized, and fortress-like qualities; Vatican II mythology, on the other hand, is outward looking and collegial.
- Because the Roman Curia remained unreformed, the euphoria of the council faded, evoking increasing grief in the people of God; the accumulated grief, which was forbidden to be mourned, turned into cultural trauma and impasse.
- Pope Francis by his actions and words is restoring the church's founding mythology, thus encouraging hope-filled mourning among the people of God.

The church is both divine and human. For this reason our Christian faith is a "treasure in clay jars" (2 Cor 4:7), that is, our faith is embedded in cultures. It is no "misty entity."[1] Every lasting human venture must express itself in identifiable symbols and institutional structures based on its founding mythology. The church is no exception. So we rightly speak of the living culture of the church in this or that parish or country or at the international level. Like every other culture the church will show signs of aging, and hopefully revitalization, globally and locally.

The impact of Vatican II on the church's culture was and continues to be profound because it radically altered the entire mythic structure of the church. Prior to the 1960s the boundaries of the fortress church had been sharply marked out and effectively patrolled lest people dare to break in or out. It was rigidly hierarchical, centralized on the pope, who

---

[1] Henri de Lubac, *The Splendour of the Church* (London: Sheed and Ward, 1956), 228.

governed the universal church through the bureaucratic
curia,[2] and his delegates, the bishops. The mythology of the
council changed all this. But the central administration of
the church, supported by sympathetic bishops, refused to
accept this. In the decades following the council it has made
repeated efforts to restore the pre-conciliar mythology. We
the people of God have been grieving over these restorationist movements. We have been forbidden to mourn the
failures to implement the council's decisions; overwhelmed
with unarticulated grief we became pastorally paralyzed
and traumatized.[3]

Then something happened to break through the impasse. An April 2014 article in the secular weekly journal
The Economist described the state of the church in early
2013 as "crisis-ridden . . . with a demoralised workforce."
But in "just a year, [it] has recovered." The author is puzzled:
how has this happened so quickly? The answer given is that
Pope Francis has refocused on the church's primary mission, namely, helping people who are poor. And, according
to the author, Francis refuses to spend time "engaging in
doctrinal disputes and staging elaborate ceremonies" and
plans the administrative restructuring of the curia.[4] The
aim of this chapter is to apply the model of the life course
of organizational cultures, explained in Chapter 5, to the
church since Vatican II and the contemporary impact of

---

[2] The Vatican curia consists of congregations possessing administrative power, tribunals having judicial authority, and offices with ministerial power. The Congregation for the Doctrine of the Faith (CDF), which
is mainly concerned with doctrinal orthodoxy, is the most influential.

[3] See Gerald A. Arbuckle, *Catholic Identity or Identities: Refounding
Ministries in Chaotic Times* (Collegeville, MN: Liturgical Press, 2013),
45–67.

[4] "The Pope as a Turnaround CEO: The Francis Effect," *The Economist*
(April 19, 2014), 10.

Francis. Francis, by the quality of his leadership, is inviting us to mourn openly for the decades of demoralization. Now we have hope that the conciliar mythology will at last become firmly embedded in the church's culture.

Model Explained

Lifecycle: Roman Catholic Church

- Stage 1: Enthusiasm, 1963–c.19.67
- Stage 2: Initial Grieving, c.1968–c.1990
- Stage 3: Grief Overload, Cultural Trauma, c.1990–2013
- Stage 4: Impasse, Extinction or Refounding, 2013–

Stage 1: Enthusiasm, 1963–c.1967

With Vatican II (1963–65) the Catholic Church came alive with new enthusiasm.[5] The council called for the refounding of the church itself. There was widespread rejoicing over the promise of a revitalized liturgy, a hope of shared leadership, and a recovery of social justice obligations. Like Washington Irving's character Rip Van Winkle, who had slept for twenty years and then awakened to a greatly changed world, the church had been oblivious of the world for five hundred years. It awoke, astonished to learn of the changes that had occurred. Everything seemed right for a massive, enthusiastic refounding of faith communities around the world based on the mythology of the church's early beginnings.

---

[5] See Gerald A. Arbuckle, *Refounding the Church: Dissent for Leadership* (Maryknoll, NY: Orbis Books, 1993), 48–60.

Stage 2: Initial Grieving, c.1968–c.1990

Once the euphoria of the council began to fade, all its inherent unaddressed weaknesses gradually became obvious. This allowed the residual pre-conciliar mythology to re-emerge with growing grief among the people of God.

Unreformed Curia

The council did not establish an appropriate process to implement its mythological changes. To fill the administrative vacuum Paul VI decided in 1967 that the unreformed curia would be responsible for the implementation of the council's major decrees.[6] The curia quickly moved to bring back the pre-conciliar mythology. Mourning rituals, such as responsible dissent, were increasingly forbidden by the curia and its supporting hierarchies around the world.[7]

The curia at the council's opening had faults characteristic of modern bureaucracies, namely, deep-seated resistance to change, lack of accountability, departmental silos that refused to collaborate, membership based on like-minded thinking, and "creeping infallibility" in administrative decisions.[8] It was vigorously criticized during the early

---

[6] See John W. O'Malley, *What Happened at Vatican II* (Cambridge, MA: The Belknap Press of Harvard University Press, 2008), 283; Hans Küng, *Can We Save the Church?* (London: William Collins, 2013), 201–05.

[7] "To start with, theological dissent is the public expression by a theologian or group of theologians of a possibility for authentic Christian experience that differs from the official formulations of the range of possibilities of that experience received from the past and defined by the magisterium of the church." See Daniel Speed Thompson, *The Language of Dissent: Edward Schillebeeckx on the Crisis of Authority in the Catholic Church* (Notre Dame, IN: University of Notre Dame Press, 2003), 151; Massimo Faggioli, *Vatican II: The Battle for Meaning* (New York: Paulist Press, 2012), 37.

[8] See Gerald A. Arbuckle, *Violence, Society, and the Church: A Cultural Approach* (Collegeville, MN: Liturgical Press, 2004), 108–11.

stages of Vatican Council II for two reasons: its bureaucratic intimidation of bishops in the past, and its attempt to manipulate the council to maintain the theologically conservative status quo.[9] The bishops refused to be bullied. The curia, on the first working day of the council, put forward 180 names for membership in the commission that would oversee the council's deliberations. The council refused to accept this interference and elected its own members.[10] However, it became clear that the curia would do whatever it could to stop or weaken reforms within itself and in the wider church. Theologian Yves Congar, OP, reported during the council that "all that was heard in the corridors of the curia were bitter complaints that 'this accursed council is ruining the church.'"[11] The curia and a minority of bishops objected to key conciliar themes such as liturgical reform, a people of God theology, reform of the curia, biblical revitalization, ecumenism, religious freedom, and the church's role in the modern world. "The idea of change in the Church was the real enemy of the council's minority."[12]

Inadequate Episcopal Leadership

A second inherent grief-evoking weakness of the council was the fact that the majority of bishops present lacked the qualities required to lead cultural changes in their dioceses

---

[9] See O'Malley, *What Happened at Vatican II*, 193; Arbuckle, *Violence, Society, and the Church*, 121–22.

[10] See Peter Hebblethwaite, *John XXIII: Pope of the Council* (London: Geoffrey Chapman, 184), 439.

[11] Yves Congar, cited in O'Malley, *What Happened at Vatican II*, 114. During the council Congar, after his appointment as a conciliar theologian, was personally warned by Cardinal Ottaviani, then in charge of the Holy Office, that he was still "under surveillance and so suspect." See Yves Congar, *My Journal of the Council* (Adelaide: ATF Theology, 2012), liii.

[12] Faggioli, *Vatican II*, 31.

according to the conciliar requirements. Before the council the primary qualification for their appointment had been their ability to maintain managerial order as shaped by centuries of tradition. Few bishops left the council aware that cultural changes of the profound nature required by the council would have to be slow and hesitant. They could not be achieved overnight by episcopal decrees.[13] As canonist Ladislas Orsy, SJ, writes: "The insights of the Council [were] so penetrating and far reaching that they [could] be grasped only slowly—even for those who took part in it. . . . To work on the unfolding of the mystery remains the task of the coming generations."[14]

Frustrated Laity and Religious

Many laity and religious—especially women—accepted the challenge to transform their lives according to the council's imperatives. They enthusiastically attended countless seminars and workshops on the mythology of the council. The more they interiorized its lessons, the more they resolved to reform the church, but they faced growing resistance from the curia and many bishops. The nineteenth century had been a period of intense growth in the number of congregations. Many founders opted for the apostolic model as developed by Saint Ignatius Loyola, but Rome kept insisting that their congregations had to adopt many inappropriate monastic and conventual customs. The dynamic founding energy of these communities was quickly suffocated by rules, for example, the requirements to wear unrealistic habits and to maintain at least a

---

[13] See Gerald A. Arbuckle, *Humanizing Healthcare Reforms* (Philadelphia: Jessica Kingsley, 2013), 14–15.

[14] Ladislas Orsy, *Receiving the Council: Theological and Canonical Insights and Debates* (Collegeville, MN: Liturgical Press, 2009), 84.

semi-cloister.[15] Their formation culture aimed to produce candidates who would loyally maintain the institutional status quo along with attitudes and behavior inimical to apostolic creativity. One could say that many apostolic communities in this era were never founded; they were forced at birth into becoming precisely what their founders did not want, namely, highly structured, rule-oriented communities ill equipped for apostolic mobility and creativity. So it was not a question of *re*founding many congregations but of *founding* them for the first time.[16] Religious set about this task with remarkable thoroughness, correctly believing that they were being true the imperatives of Vatican II. Tensions and much grief developed as the gap widened between committed religious and unreformed bishops and the curia.

Dissent Discouraged

In 1968, three years after the council ended, Paul VI published the encyclical *Humanae vitae,* reasserting the teachings of Pius XI and Pius XII banning the use of artificial birth-control methods. This caused further worldwide distress both inside and outside the church.[17] Massimo Faggioli, reflecting on the impact of *Humanae vitae* on the church, wrote that it "inaugurated the disillusionment

---

[15] For example, religious women had to wear woolen religious habits designed for the colder climates of Europe in bitterly hot and rainy tropical countries such as Africa. In the South Pacific islands religious sisters were expected to wear these heavy habits even when attempting to negotiate treacherous surf in small, frail landing boats. We can only guess at the amount of sickness among religious caused by this very foolish rule.

[16] See Gerald A. Arbuckle, *From Chaos to Mission: Refounding Religious Life Formation* (Collegeville, MN: Liturgical Press, 1995), 27–28.

[17] See Peter Hebblewhaite, *Paul VI: The First Modern Pope* (New York: Paulist Press, 1993), 505–26.

of the post–Vatican II era." It represented the start of the division between the magisterium and a theology that abandoned "metaphysics as its center of orientation and increasingly [became] a theology of 'salvation history,' where human history also becomes a real source of theological work."[18] Paul VI, preaching on June 29, 1972, highlighted the growing grief at all levels of the church: "After the Council, we believed there would be a day of sunshine in the history of the Church. Instead there arrived a day of clouds, of tempest, of darkness, of questioning, of uncertainty."[19] Historian Peter Hebblewhaite strongly argues that Paul VI "never wavered in his commitment to the full implementation of Vatican II."[20] Nevertheless, his failure to reform the curia would increasingly haunt the church.[21]

Theologians began to voice their growing anxiety at the curia's obstructive behavior and bemoaned lost opportunities to implement the council's vision for the church. In 1974 Karl Rahner, SJ, forthrightly wrote that "there is no Christian principle to the effect that the conservatives must always be right when a choice has to be made" between the curia and its supporters and future-oriented people.[22] In 1982 theologian Avery Dulles (later a cardinal) sadly

---

[18] Faggioli, *Vatican II,* 133.

[19] The English translation of the homily appears, among other places, in Nicholas Lash, *Theology for Pilgrims* (Notre Dame, IN: University of Notre Dame Press, 2008), 259. An official English translation of the homily is not available.

[20] Hebblewhaite, *Paul VI,* 7.

[21] See John R. Quinn, *The Reform of the Papacy* (New York: Crossroad, 1999), 154–77. Thomas Reese described in 1998 the negative qualities of the curia: "Arrogance, ambition, careerism, cronyism, legalism, and politics are all alive in the Vatican," in *Inside the Vatican* (Cambridge, MA: Harvard University Press, 1998), 170.

[22] Karl Rahner, *The Shape of the Church to Come* (New York: Seabury Press, 1974), 49.

expressed his concern that the hierarchal church was failing to be collegial:

> Without minimizing the charismatic gifts of official leaders [in the church], we may acknowledge that, in a sinful world, those who hold office will commonly be tempted to employ their power in a dominative and manipulative way. They can easily tend to sacrifice other values to the demands of law and order and to misconceive of loyalty as if it meant merely passive conformity.[23]

The revised Code of Canon Law promulgated in 1983 also clearly sent the message to the universal church that Rome was turning its back on the council. Orsy noted in 1991 that the revised code "offers little or no help for [the] evolution of [particular churches] and we are all the poorer for it."[24] Rome weakened the authority of the episcopal conferences and the bishops' synod; the new code speaks about the collaborative rights of episcopal conferences in about ninety places, but on careful evaluation it is clear that allowances for decentralization are outweighed by the emphasis given to the role of Rome. For example, the US Episcopal Conference in 1983 was told by Rome that it did not have the skills to write a pastoral letter on peace.[25]

---

[23] Avery Dulles, *A Church to Believe In: Discipleship and the Dynamics of Freedom* (New York: Crossroads, 1982), 36–37.

[24] Ladislas Orsy, "The Revision of Canon Law," in *Modern Catholicism: Vatican II and After*, ed. Adrian Hastings (London: SPCK, 1991), 22. See also Knut Walf, "The New Canon Law—The Same Old System: Preconciliar Spirit in Postconciliar Formulatio," in *The Church in Anguish: Has the Vatican Betrayed Vatican II?* ed. Hans Küng and Leonard Swidler (San Francisco: Harper and Row, 1986), 90.

[25] See Peter Hebblethwaite, "The Pope and the Bishops," *The Tablet* (April 30, 1983).

The 1985 Extraordinary Synod met to evaluate the role of the council in the postconciliar church, but "its abandonment of 'the People of God' as the key concept in understanding the Church and its 'pessimistic' re-editing of 'the signs of the times' [were] further evidence of the dismantling of the heritage of Paul VI"[26] and the council, thus evoking more disappointment and sadness in the church. Cardinal Joseph Ratzinger (later Pope Benedict XVI) published an evaluation in 1985 of the post–Vatican II church that initiated further alarm and grief among evangelizers committed to a culture of openness and apostolic boldness within the church. Even allowing for obvious excesses following the council, the emotive and condemnatory expressions he used of the postconciliar years are disturbing, for example, a period of "self-destruction," "discouragement" and "decadence." The model of the church as the people of God caused him anxiety, as did the prominence being given to the teaching role of episcopal conferences. He highlighted the relevance using the threat of excommunication as a way ultimately to control theologians or others judged to be endangering the "purity" of the church's teaching and boundaries.[27] Overall, there was a negativity and an undisguised fear of the new throughout his book. He said nothing about the need to interact with the postmodern world or the role of prophetic persons and institutions that risk the new for the building of the kingdom.

Saint John Paul II was indeed most zealous and tireless in his efforts to preach the word. Yet his image of the church was hierarchically vertical or pyramidal according to the preconciliar model. On the one hand, he exhorted Catholics to

---

[26] Hebblethwaite, *Paul VI*, 7.

[27] See Joseph Ratzinger with Vittorio Messori, *The Ratzinger Report: An Exclusive Interview on the State of the Church* (San Francisco: Ignatius Press, 1985), 28, 48–49, 24–26.

be bold in preaching the gospel (*Redemptoris missio*, no. 87), but it was to be a boldness *within* the rule-oriented structures of a static ecclesiastical culture. The ethos of negativity within the church (*RM*, no. 36) that he complained about, however, was mainly a result of his overemphasis on the outdated model of the church. But apostolic boldness was impossible in a church in which people became increasingly fearful of being reported to bishops and the Roman Curia for daring to devise urgently needed pastoral strategies.[28]

Fundamentalism Encouraged

As the chaos continued to develop in the church, restorationist movements—with their hopes for a return to a utopian past, that is, to a church purified of "dangerous ideas and practices"—began to flourish. While movements such as the Neocatechumenal Way, Opus Dei, and Communion and Liberation have been encouraged by Rome and have spiritually benefited many people, nonetheless they contain significant restorationist qualities.[29]

In summary, in the years that followed the council the Vatican centralized bureaucracy increasingly dominated the control of the church. Consequently, as Eamon Duffy has correctly observed, the world's bishops became subjugated to a "managerial papacy."[30] Among the people of God the symptoms of unarticulated grief, such as bewilderment, sadness, anger, fatalism, shame over the internal divisions in the church, a sense of powerlessness and growing cynicism, intensified widely. Sociologist Sister Augusta Neal summarized the growing frustration and sadness of religious women in 1990:

---

[28] See Arbuckle, *Refounding the Church*, 59–60.

[29] See Arbuckle, *Violence, Society, and the Church*, 208–13.

[30] Eamon Duffy, "Style Is Not Enough," *The Tablet* (March 8, 2014). Duffy is professor of the history of Christianity at Cambridge University.

Many Catholic sisters faced a serious dilemma of obedience in the 1980s and will continue to do so in the 1990s. This dilemma takes the form of a conflict between honoring Vatican Council mandates to prophetic ministry and resuming the traditional form of the vow of obedience in the practice of submission to the will of a specific person in a position of authority.[31]

Stage 3: Grief Overload, Cultural Trauma, c.1990–2013

> *"We were far too hesitant. I beat my own breast here. We certainly lacked the courage to speak out openly."*
> —Cardinal Christoph Schonborn,
> "Pope Francis Has Already
> Changed Church"

Four events combined to form the tipping point that led to this stage of grief overload and cultural trauma: the publication of the document *Liturgiam authenticam;* the publicity relating to the worldwide abuse scandals in the church, both sexual and financial (for example, corruption in the Vatican Bank); the scapegoating within the church; and the controversial imposing of new translations of the Roman Missal.

Liturgiam authenticam

In 2001 Rome issued *Liturgiam authenticam,* a document firmly asserting that Rome has the right to intervene in liturgical matters. It undermines the center of Vatican II ecclesiology by further centralizing power in the curia and by demanding that local cultures implement an essentially

---

[31] Mary Augusta Neal, *From Nuns to Sisters: An Expanding Vocation* (Mystic, CT: Twenty-Third Publications, 1990), 89.

Roman form of worship.[32] The curia-centered control is not confined to liturgical matters only but is to embrace all aspects that relate to faith and culture, including such matters as interreligious dialogue and social justice. Not surprisingly, Father Michael Amaladoss, SJ, director of the Institute of Dialogue with Cultures and Religions in India, concludes that "the process of inculturation is not making much headway in the Church today because it is mostly seen as the translation and adaptation of a pre-existent 'pure' gospel" that has a "privileged and normative expression in Judaic and Greco-Roman cultures."[33]

Abuse Scandals

In the early 1990s the sexual-abuse scandals, including the cover-ups by Rome and bishops began to hit the media and have continued ever since.[34] Not only anger and compassion for the victims but also an ever-increasing sense of shame have become the daily part of a grieving church. Trust was broken. Morale was shattered, resulting in thousands leaving the church. Rome's moral integrity and credibility were undermined.[35] The church is now clearly seen to lack the

---

[32] See John L. Allen, "New Document Replaces Thirty-Five Years of Liturgy Work," *National Catholic Reporter* (May 25, 2001).

[33] Michael Amaladoss, "Liturgical Inculturation and Postmodern Culture," *East Asian Pastoral Review* 44 (2007). Also see Gerald A. Arbuckle, *Culture, Inculturation, and Theologians: A Postmodern Critique* (Collegeville, MN: Liturgical Press, 2010), 138–51, 177–79.

[34] See Philip Jenkins, *Pedophiles and Priests: Anatomy of a Contemporary Crisis* (Oxford: Oxford University Press, 1996), 46–47.

[35] The bishops of New Zealand, in their address to the pope in 1998, reflected the ongoing frustration of many episcopal conferences: "Within the household of the Catholic Church itself, Discasteries [curia] of the Holy See occasionally make norms which impinge on the ministry of bishops with little or no consultation of the episcopate as such. This seems inconsistent." Bishop Peter J. Cullinane, "A Time to Speak Out," *The Tablet* (November 22, 1998).

transparency and accountability demanded by the council, a church "more concerned with protecting the reputation of the institution and the clerical profession than in safeguarding real or potential child victims."[36] Even George Weigel, a very conservative observer, complained that "the People of God are treated as if they were cattle, not sheep to be nourished and shepherded."[37] When the cardinals met in 2005, they urged as a priority the reform of the curia, but this reform did not take place under Benedict XVI; the situation further deteriorated during his pontificate.[38] John Thavis commented that Benedict XVI "faced with actual evidence of impropriety and infighting in his own city-state . . . appeared uninterested."[39] Thavis described the bureaucratic dysfunctionality in the curia with its silo mentality as

> a patchwork of departments, communities and individuals, all loosely bound by a sense of mission but without comprehensive management or rigorous oversight . . . where each agency of the Roman Curia jealously guards its turf, where the little guys and big shots may work at cross-purposes and where slipups and misunderstandings are common.[40]

Examples of this organizational sickness became sadly evident: the lengthy delay, despite the extent of the evidence available, in admitting the scandalous behavior of Marcial Degollado Maciel, founder of the Legion of Christ; the failure to research Bishop Richard Williamson's background

---

[36] Jenkins, *Pedophiles and Priests,* 3–4.
[37] George Weigel, *Evangelical Catholicism: Deep Reform in the Twenty-First Century Church* (New York: Basic Books, 2013), 251.
[38] Ibid., 250.
[39] John Thavis, *The Vatican Diaries* (London: Penguin, 2013), 302.
[40] Ibid., 5.

as a member of the schismatic Society of Saint Pius X; the side-lining of Archbishop Carlo Maria Vigano, secretary-general of the Vatican City, who had sought to achieve much needed reforms in the scandal-prone Vatican Bank.

Scapegoating Within the Church

Three groups within the church that are relatively powerless are women, theologians, and people who are poor.[41] For this reason they are in constant danger of becoming the objects of ecclesiastical witch hunting. In 2009 Cardinal Franc Rode, prefect of the Congregation for Religious, was deputed by Benedict XVI to lead a review of American women's religious communities. Thousands of women religious who had loyally given their lives to frontline evangelization, often with minimal financial support, were under suspicion by Rome. Many are elderly and not infrequently living close to the poverty line. However, the months' long investigation lost momentum when pictures were published of the cardinal robed in a medieval, expensive scarlet *capa magna* ordaining deacons. The contrast between the cardinal's symbols of monarchical power and prestige was in vivid contrast to the simple lifestyles of the religious women. Then, in 2012, the CDF announced that it would begin an assessment of the theological orthodoxy of the LCWR (Leadership Conference of Women Religious). This decision was made without consultation with or even the knowledge of Cardinal Braz de Aviz, prefect of the Congregation for Institutes of Consecrated Life and Societies of Apostolic

---

[41] See Daniel S. Thompson, *The Language of Dissent: Edward Schillebeeckx on the Crisis of Authority in the Catholic Church* (Notre Dame, IN: University of Notre Dame Press, 2003), 1–9; Bradford E. Hinze, "A Decade of Disciplining Theologians," in *When the Magisterium Intervenes: The Magisterium and Theologians in Today's Church*, ed. Richard R. Gaillardetz (Collegeville, MN: Liturgical Press, 2012), 3–39; Arbuckle, *Violence, Society, and the Church*, 144–46.

Life—a sad example of bureaucratic compartmentalization or siloism.

Writing about theologians, James Provost, then professor of canon law at the Catholic University of America, wrote in 1989: "The rejection of any type of 'dissent' from non-infallible positions has been severe, despite the exception made for many years in the case of Archbishop Lefebvre. There has been an on-going harassment of theologians . . . which often appears as an attempt to appease influential minorities." Provost comments that the way this authority is being used on occasions "has the appearance of a defensive effort to exercise centralized control—defensive against the 'evil' world in contrast to the Second Vatican Council's views . . . defensive of a very limited school of theology."[42] This harassment of theologians continued through Pope Benedict's pontificate.

As in all witch hunts, the respect for truth and human rights can be ignored, as the following description of the judicial process formed by the CDF shows.[43] It remains substantially unaltered since it was inaugurated in 1971:[44]

---

[42] James Provost, "The Papacy: Power, Authority, Leadership," in *The Papacy and the Church in the United States*, ed. Bernard Cooke (New York: Paulist Press, 1989), 205.

[43] For further explanation, see Arbuckle, *Catholic Identity or Identities*, 15–20.

[44] The Holy See published new rules in 1997, called "Regulations for the Examination of Doctrines," which modified existing norms governing the scrutiny of theologians. However, these rules do not substantially change the previous rules. As canonist Ladislas Orsy writes: "for anyone educated in the sensitivities of jurisprudence, [they] do not respond, as they were intended, to the demands of the present day. . . . They have their roots in past ages; they were not born from the vision of human dignity and the respect for honest conscience that is demanded the world over today. . . . They are not rooted in any divine precept" (*Receiving the Council*, 102–3). Theologian Elizabeth Johnson had not heard that the Committee on Doctrine of the United States Bishops Conference had examined and rigorously criticized her book *Quest for the Living God*

The CDF is prosecutor, judge, and jury; persons being investigated are not told of the inquiry until stage thirteen (of eighteen stages) and may never know the identity of their accusers; defendants are unable to choose their defenders or even know their identity, nor is there access to material relating to the allegations against the accused; no publicity is permitted concerning the proceedings; and there is no right of appeal.[45] Serious injustices can happen. For the CDF secrecy is important in the judicial process. Secrecy is a powerful weapon of control in witch hunting, and it is a particular quality of hierarchical cultures. It is a way for elites to maintain power through the possession of special knowledge and for non-elites to protect themselves from the obtrusive interference of the elites.[46] In 2009 Orsy repeated his concerns that creative theologians were in constant fear of being silenced and that this endangered the church's future: "Creative thinkers are one of the greatest assets of our church: they let the internal riches of the evangelical message unfold."[47] In brief, the task now assigned to theologians became increasingly reduced to explaining the authoritative pronouncements of the official church. This is a return to pre–Vatican II practice.

Theologian Father Charles Curran, when assessing in 2012 the growing censuring of theologians and anyone who

---

until the day prior to the publication of their document. She had never been invited to meet and dialogue with the committee (see Richard R. Gaillardetz, "The Elizabeth Johnson Dossier," in Gaillardetz, *When the Magisterium Intervenes*, 178).

[45] This description comes from moral theologian B. Quelquejeu and is quoted in Richard A. McCormick and Richard P. O'Brien, "L'Affaire Curran II," *America* 163/6 (1990): 128.

[46] See Donald N. Levine, *The Flight from Ambiguity: Essays in Social and Cultural Theory* (Chicago: University of Chicago Press, 1985), 33; Gerald A. Arbuckle, *Confronting the Demon: A Gospel Response to Adult Bullying* (Collegeville, MN: Liturgical Press, 2003), 65–94.

[47] Orsy, *Receiving the Council*, 103.

questions Rome's authoritarian decision-making processes, concludes that it is now only concerned to maintain

> a remnant church—a small and pure church that sees itself often in opposition to the world around it. . . . This concept of the church is opposed to the best understanding of the Catholic Church. . . . The church embraces both saints and sinners, rich and poor, female and male, and political conservatives and liberals. Yes, there are limits to what it means to be a Catholic, but the "small 'c' catholic" understanding insists on the need to be as inclusive as possible.[48]

Roman Missal Translation

Finally, for many Catholics frustration with monarchical Rome reached a breaking point in 2010 when it imposed a new English translation of the Roman Missal on the English-speaking world.[49] Rome refused to listen not only to angry experts in the English language, but also to believers in the pews who found the translation often archaic and not infrequently unintelligible. Not only is the language exclusive, but the translation slavishly follows the Latin

---

[48] Charles Curran, "Condemnation of 'Just Love' Not a Surprise in This Day and Age," *National Catholic Reporter* (June 6, 2012). See also John L. Allen, who thinks that Benedict XVI no longer believed in the notion of a remnant church, that is, a church that is smaller in order to be more pure. To support his view, Allen cites Benedict's commitment to New Evangelization, which aims to draw lapsed Catholics back to the church in the Western world and to reach out to others who feel alienated by postmodernity ("Benedict XVI a Pope of Ironies," *National Catholic Reporter* (April 20, 2012).

[49] See Philip Endean, "Worship and Power," *The Tablet* (August 28, 2010); Peter J. Cullinane, "Liturgy and the Role of Bishops," *The Tablet* (July 30, 2011), 17–18; R. Kevin Seasoltz, *A Virtuous Church: Catholic Theology, Ethics, and Liturgy for the Twenty-First Century* (Maryknoll, NY: Orbis Books, 2012), 200.

style of long sentences broken up into numerous clauses. Justly, Duffy writes of "craven acquiescence of the English-speaking conferences [of bishops] in the ghastly translation of the Missal which now afflicts us."[50]

In summary, by the beginning of 2013 the church was unquestionably suffering from grief overload and cultural trauma. Anthropologist Mary Douglas describes one particular model of culture, which she terms *strong group/strong grid*,[51] that helps to explain the nature of the culture Rome had been trying to reimpose on the people of God. In this model the boundaries of the culture and the way individuals are to relate to one another within these boundaries are rigidly defined and maintained.[52] The wider world of change has to be kept at bay for fear that it will destroy the purity of the culture. Orthodoxy means that people are expected to fit into a tradition-based, bureaucratic, hierarchical, and patriarchal system. Dress codes insist on formality. The cosmology of the culture mirrors and reinforces this static system. Identities are normative;[53] that is, they are imposed by tradition and are commonly reduced in practice to one dominant identity, namely, unquestioning submission to the status quo. Since responsible dissent is forbidden, those who dare to do so are marginalized. They become "non-people." Since the role of official leaders is to maintain the status quo, they emphasize ceremonies or formal displays of power structures, not rituals. Ceremonies

---

[50] Duffy, "Style Is Not Enough," 7.

[51] See particularly the following studies by Mary Douglas: *Natural Symbols: Explorations in Cosmology* (New York: Pantheon Books, 1970), and *Purity and Danger: An Analysis of the Concepts of Pollution and Taboo* (London: Routledge and Kegan Paul, 1966).

[52] For a fuller explanation of this model as applied to the church, see Arbuckle, *Refounding the Church*, 80–85.

[53] See Arbuckle, *Catholic Identity or Identities*, 3–4.

and spectacles celebrate and reinforce the cultural status quo; rituals—for example, rituals of mourning—transform the status quo.[54]

Many among the people of God felt increasingly betrayed by this Roman cultural imperialism yet are forbidden to lament publicly over the substantial failures of the institutional church to live up to the vision of the council. And the shame resulting from the publication of more and more scandals—both sexual and institutional—has evoked an ever-deepening collective depression characteristic of cultural trauma. Hans Küng concluded that the church was in such suppressed grief that it was now suffering from a "debilitating and potentially terminal illness."[55] Anthropologically, he is correct. Vatican II had theoretically returned the church to the mythology of the gospel, raising the expectations of the people of God. Yet the more the institutional church encouraged the mythology of the pre-counciliar era to resurface, the more people, if they remained in the church, were tempted to despair. Those who had deeply imbibed the council's vision felt increasingly betrayed, forbidden to lament and mourn publicly over the massive failures of the institutional church to live up to the vision of the council. For those who still lived in hope, the prayer of the psalmist in old age was on their lips (see Chapter 1):

---

[54] Victor Turner distinguishes ritual from ceremony: "Ritual is transformative, ceremony confirmatory" (*The Forest of Symbols: Aspects of Ndembu* [Ithaca, NY: Cornell University Press, 1976], 164). Ceremonies confirm and reinforce the pre-existing order of statuses/roles; rituals are concerned with the change in statuses/roles. Turner sees that ritual is the temporary suspension of social hierarchies, the remaking of personal identities, and the stimulation of cultural creativity (Arbuckle, *Culture, Inculturation, and Theologians*, 81–98).

[55] Hans Küng, *Can We Save the Catholic Church?* (London: William Collins, 2013), 1.

> In you, O LORD, I take refuge;
>   let me never be put to shame. . . .
>   Incline your ear to me and save me. . . .
> For you, O LORD, are my hope,
>   my trust, O LORD, from my youth.
>
> (Ps 71:1, 2, 5)

Stage 4: Impasse, Extinction or Refounding, 2013–

Extinction at this stage can mean either radical numerical decline or, more important, what I call "disintegration of the heart" among the people of God. While there is definitely no global decline in the church, nonetheless in significant parts of the church there is reason for concern. For example, among United States citizens, 10 percent are ex-Catholics, and for every convert the church gains, four leave; in Brazil the church is losing the faithful at an accelerating rate to myriad evangelical Protestant churches and to atheism.[56] "Disintegration of the heart" means the intense, paralyzing, collective grief among the people of God that the church had lost its way, an almost despairing sense that there was no longer a passion for the gospel and ministry, cynicism and distrust of the hierarchy, and overwhelming shame as more and more scandals were revealed—a widespread loss of hope in the future. Then something totally unforeseen and remarkable occurred to break this impasse and to re-vitalize hope in the people of God—the election of Pope Francis. It is as though God has inclined his ear and saved

---

[56] See *The Economist* (July 30, 2013), 37, and (March 29, 2014), 31. In the United States only "55% of Latinos call themselves Catholic, a drop of 12 points in three years. The decline is steeper among 18- to 29-year olds. . . . Most youngsters who fall away no longer claim any religious affiliation" (*The Economist* [May 17, 2014], 35).

the people of God (Ps 71) from the devastating darkness of the cultural trauma and impasse into which the church had sunk. The residual founding mythology of the church itself, not the pre-conciliar mythology, has dramatically begun to resurface under the leadership of Pope Francis, a wisdom figure. Through his many actions and words he is leading the church in a massive ritual of letting go of attachments to a monarchical papacy and its theological foundations. The people of God have permission at last to mourn publicly. At the same time he aims to avoid the trap of not building governance structures to ensure Vatican II mythology is firmly embedded in the church's culture.

Francis has an extraordinary ability to communicate his ideas and those of the gospel purely by gesture. From the moment of his election he adopted a new style of leadership based on the founding mythology of the church: "unlike his predecessor, no miter with gold and jewels, no ermine-trimmed cape, no made-to-measure red shoes and head-wear, no magnificent throne." Even an outsider, Elton John, comments: "Francis is a miracle of humility in an era of vanity. . . . This pope seems to want to bring the Church back to the ancient values of Christ and at the same time [bring it into] the 21st century."[57] And he "deliberately abstains from solemn gestures and high-flown rhetoric and speaks the language of the people."[58] By his words and behavior he has said a definite no to deadening restorationism with its insistence on coercive rules and an unambiguous yes to being involved in the hopes and frustrations of people and their cultures:

---

[57] Mary Katherine Haley, "Sir Elton John Says Pope Francis Is 'A Miracle of Humility,'" *Catholic Herald* (July 10, 2013).

[58] Hans Küng, "The Paradox of Pope Francis," *National Catholic Reporter* (May 21, 2013).

If the Christian is a restorationist, a legalist, if he wants everything clear and safe, then he will find nothing. . . . Those who today always look for disciplinarian solutions, those who long for an exaggerated doctrinal "security," those who stubbornly try to recover a past that no longer exists—they have a static and inward-directed view of things. . . . God is in every person's life. Even if the life of a person has been a disaster . . . You must try to seek God in every human life. Although the life of a person is a land full of thorns and weeds, there is always a space in which the good seed can grow. You have to trust God.[59]

A church that is fearful of the world becomes a church of protective rules, a fortress church of the pre-conciliar type. Francis will have none of this. As cardinal he said that the church had become "too wrapped up in itself . . . too navel-gazing . . . 'self-referential'" and that this had "made it sick . . . suffering a 'kind of theological narcissism.'"[60] As pope he wrote: "I prefer a Church which is bruised, hurting and dirty because it has been out in the streets, rather than a Church that is unhealthy from being confined and from clinging to its own security" (*Evangelii gaudium*, no. 49). Neither the church nor the evangelizer is to be the focus of our concern, but rather the "center is Jesus Christ, who

---

[59] Antonio Spadaro, SJ, "A Big Heart Open to God," interview with Pope Francis, *America* (September 30, 2013), www.americamagazine. org/pope-interview.

[60] Cardinal Jorge Bergoglio to cardinals meeting in conclave, cited in Paul Vallely, *Pope Francis: Untying the Knots* (London: Bloomsbury, 2013), 155. During the Easter rituals in 2013 Francis warned the clergy against becoming mere "managers" or "antique collectors" obsessed with liturgical niceties, urging them to leave their sacristies to change the secular world. See William Pfaff, "Challenge to the Church," *The New York Review of Books* (May 9, 2013), 11.

calls us and sends us forth."[61] The church's primary task is to evangelize, not to protect itself from the sufferings of others especially people who are poor and vulnerable:

> "Mere administration" can no longer be enough. . . . I dream of a "missionary option," that is, a missionary impulse capable of transforming everything, so that the Church's customs, ways of doing things, times and schedules, language and structures can be suitably channeled for the evangelization of today's world rather than for her self-preservation. (*EG*, nos. 25, 27)

Francis's primary model of the church, therefore, is not hierarchical but the people of God: "The image of the church I like is that of the holy, faithful people of God. . . . There is no full identity without belonging to a people."[62] And Francis expresses this identity personally by openly proclaiming that he too is a sinner. Little wonder that Francis is such a powerful communicator. People feel he understands them.

Given the theological foundations of Francis's thinking, it is inevitable that he has courageously begun the structural reform of the curia and has promised a collegial approach to decision making. The latter is evident, for example, in his decision that in the preparation for the Synod on the Family the voices of the people of God should be heard.[63]

---

[61] Quoted in Thomas Reese, "Pope Francis' Ecclesiology Rooted in the Emmaus Story," *National Catholic Reporter* (August 6, 2013).

[62] Francis, quoted in Spadaro, "A Big Heart Open to God."

[63] The rift between the CDF and the LCWR (USA) remains, but the representatives of the latter noted a welcome change in the manner in which the CDF and other Vatican offices receive them: "Monsignor Paul Tigue, Secretary, shared that Pope Francis insists upon creating, as part of the New Evangelization, a culture of encounter, marked by dialogue and discernment. We experienced this culture of encounter in every Vatican office we visited in the Curia, an encounter marked by genuine

He has also named the initial members of a commission to advise him on sexual-abuse policy, drawing on lay and religious experts, including an Irish woman assaulted as a child by a priest.[64]

Culture and Inculturation

Francis has a particularly sensitive feeling for the power and importance of cultures. A culture is not something static or mechanistic. Rather, it "is a dynamic reality which a people constantly recreates" (*EG*, no. 122). For this reason he forthrightly believes in inculturation, namely, the need to begin theology with the realities of people's lives, their hearts, and their cultures. Inculturation has too long meant in papal thinking that all cultures must adapt to a Roman-centered view of the church.[65] In this Francis is perfectly allied with great theologians of the church and the council's refounding mythology. Certain church fathers, such as Justin, Irenaeus, and Clement of Alexandria, either explicitly or implicitly speak about the seeds sown by the word of God in cultures.[66] Justin claims: "Everything good that has been said, no matter by whom, is Christian."[67] The word of God is actively present, although in an incomplete way, in all cultures. This presence

---

interaction and mutual respect." Thomas Fox, "LCWR on Accusations: 'Communication Has Broken Down'; 'Mistrust Has Developed'," *National Catholic Reported* (May 8, 2014).

[64] See "The Catholic Church and Child Abuse," *The Economist* (May 17, 2014), 53–54.

[65] See Arbuckle, *Culture, Inculturation, and Theologians*, 138–51.

[66] See Pontifical Council for Inter-Religious Dialogue and the Congregation for the Evangelization of Peoples, "Dialogue and Proclamation," *Origins* 21/8 (July 4, 1991), 125.

[67] Justin the Martyr, cited in Leonardo Boff, *Church, Charism, and Power: Liberation Theology and the Institutional Church* (London: SCM Press, 1985), 94.

or glimmer of the transcendence is the foreshadowing of the fuller revelation of Jesus Christ in the scriptures and tradition. Whatever is good in cultures comes from the Spirit.[68] As Karl Rahner writes, "The very commonness of everyday things harbours the eternal marvel and silent mystery of God and his grace."[69] Francis thus challenges theologians to "always remember that the Church and theology exist to evangelize, and not be content with a desk-bound theology" (*EG*, no. 133).

One indication of Francis's commitment to inculturation is his emphasis on the need to accept popular piety as a foundation for people's faith and religious practice in many parts of the world. Quoting from the Fifth General Conference of the Latin American and Caribbean Bishops, he writes that it is "a legitimate way of living the faith, a way of feeling part of the Church and a manner of being missionaries" (*EG*, no. 124). He concludes: "Let us not stifle or presume to control this missionary power!" (*EG*, no. 124). Theologians have commonly looked down upon popular piety believing it is an imperfect faith, even dangerous to theological thinking and practice.[70] Not so Francis! Popular piety is "a true expression of the spontaneous missionary activity of the people of God. This is an ongoing and developing process, of which the Holy Spirit is the principal agent" (*EG*, no. 122).

A further indication of Francis's respect for cultures was the challenge he gave to representatives of the Neocatechumenal Way, a restorationist movement in the church. After

---

[68] For a fuller description of this mystery, see Gerald A. Arbuckle, *Laughing with God: Humor, Culture, and Transformation* (Collegeville, MN: Liturgical Press, 2008), 111–13.

[69] Karl Rahner, *Belief Today* (London: Sheed and Ward, 1973), 4.

[70] See Arbuckle, *Culture, Inculturation, and Theologians*, 183–88.

encouraging them as his predecessors had done, Francis then significantly reminded them that "God and the Holy Spirit has already preceded them" in the cultures they wish to evangelize.[71] The movement has long believed that until cultures are evangelized, they are evil; there is nothing of God in the different ways people express themselves in their cultures. Francis counseled them to cease imposing their distinctively Spanish-Italian model of the church and worship on other cultures. Given his emphasis on incultura-tion, it is not surprising that Francis has reinstated the role of the social sciences as a means to better understand the complexity of cultures and how they can assist the process of pastoral discernment.[72] Contrary to conciliar thinking, Rome had become increasingly suspicious of these sciences.

In the Gospels we see Jesus Christ as the master of in-culturation. The people of his time yearn in the midst of the political and economic chaos for teachers who speak their language. Jesus does this through the simplicity and wisdom of stories or parables that mirror people's experi-ence, for example, stories about the arrogance of the rich, the pomposity and corruption of officials, rowdy neighbors, the problems of bringing up adolescent children, poor widows. Then there are straightforward words of wisdom about living well, for example, the advice Jesus offers in his Sermon on the Mount. Francis does likewise. People in our postmodern world also thirst for leaders who can with sin-cerity relate to their deepest concerns and in language they can understand, people whose lives witness to the wisdom they speak.[73] Francis is such a leader, for example, in his

---

[71] "Pope to Neo-cats: Respect Local Cultures," *The Tablet* (February 8, 2014).

[72] Ibid.

[73] See Arbuckle, *Catholic Identity or Identities*, 130–39, 173–245.

tender references to the influence of his grandmother Rosa and in the easy manner in which he retells gospel stories.[74]

In summary, the church must be a mission-driven culture, says Francis. The mission of Jesus Christ to the world demands that individuals and institutions are constantly evaluating structures and customs in terms of this mission. The culture model that Francis desires for the church is what Mary Douglas describes as *weak group/ weak grid*.[75] This is a mission-driven culture, a pilgrim culture, in which members commit themselves to work together for the common good. Group belonging and structures exist to serve the mission, not vice versa as in a *strong group/strong grid* culture. Though there are different roles and ranks in this culture model, there are strong egalitarian and gender qualities to how people relate to one another simply because they share a common external mission. Thus, if a structure no longer serves the mission, it needs to change, and people need to be willing to do so. Decisions are made, wherever possible, through dialogue. Identities are *normative* and especially *dynamic*, that is, individuals and institutions must forever be negotiating identities in the light of existing norms and changing circumstances.[76]

---

[74] In his Palm Sunday homily in the midst of the grandeur of Saint Peter's Square in 2013 Francis said: "Our grandmother used to say: 'a shroud has no pockets.'" This was a simple way of saying that we cannot take our possessions with us in death.

[75] See Arbuckle, *Refounding the Church*, 90–93.

[76] See Arbuckle, *Catholic Identity or Identities*, 5–12. Anthony Giddens calls this process of negotiating identities an exercise of the "reflexive self," that is, a process whereby "self-identity is constituted by the reflexive ordering of self-narratives." *The Transformation of Intimacy: Sexuality, Love, and Eroticism in Modern Societies* (Cambridge: Polity, 1992), 75.

Responsible Dissent

In June 2014 the International Theological Commission published a document approved by Cardinal Gerhard Muller, head of the CDF, entitled *"Sensus Fidei* in the Life of the Church."[77] Its pastoral tone reflects the reforming influence of Pope Francis and his desire to discourage an authoritarian approach to theological discussion. While understandably naming the magisterium as having the ultimate say, the document openly accepts the importance of, and reasons for, responsible dissent in the church. "Alerted by their *sensus fidei,* individual believers may deny assent even to the teaching of legitimate pastors if they do not recognize in that teaching the voice of Christ, the Good Shepherd" (no. 63).

The denial of assent can be due to failures on both sides:

> There are occasions, however, when the reception of magisterial teaching by the faithful meets with difficulty and resistance, and appropriate action on both sides is required in such situations. . . . The magisterium must . . . reflect on the teaching that has been given and consider whether it needs clarification or reformulation in order to communicate more effectively the essential message. (no. 80)

The document later says: "In some cases [indifference or dissent] may indicate that certain decisions have been taken by those in authority without due consideration of the experience and the *sensus fidei* of the faithful, or without

---

[77] International Theological Commission, *Sensus Fidei in the Life of the Church,* www.vatican.va/roman_curia/congregations/cfaith/cti_documents/rc_cti_20140610_sensus-fidei_en.html.

sufficient consultation of the faithful by the magisterium" (no. 123). Finally, "Humble listening at all levels and proper consultation of those concerned are integral aspects of a living and lively church" (no. 126).

Francis: A Gospel Comedian

I believe we can speak of Francis as a gospel comedian. All good comedians, such as King Lear's Fool, and in the early days of the movies, Charlie Chaplin, have one thing in common. They refuse to be dominated by the haughtiness and self-importance of the high and mighty. In fact, such figures become objects of amusement and even pity.[78] True comedians are able to touch the hearts of their audiences. We feel they understand and empathize with us. They are liminal people, projecting in their behavior society's fundamental paradoxes such as hope and despair, order and disorder. Yet they are able at the same time to rise above these incongruities. They purposely create disorder in the midst of order to give the appearance of incongruity. They call us into this incongruous situation to experience its tensions and then invite us to resolve them. Their message? The social status quo is not set in concrete.[79]

Mary Douglas describes comedians as "ritual purifiers." She even proposes that "perhaps the joker should be classed as a kind of minor mystic."[80] Comedians invite their audiences to critique orderly structures and status in society in search of deeper values and truths about

---

[78] See Conrad Hyers, *The Comic Vision and the Christian Faith: A Celebration of Life and Laughter* (New York: Pilgrim Press, 1991), 64–65.

[79] For a fuller explanation of these insights, see Arbuckle, *Laughing with God*, 52–55.

[80] Mary Douglas, *Purity and Danger: An Analysis of Concepts of Pollution and Taboo* (Harmondsworth: Penguin, 1966), 108.

life. Good comedians mock on behalf of humanity the behavior of those who unduly assert authority, who overly insist on rules and obedience to traditions. They do not just condemn the world of status, wealth, power, and violence, but in some way they give us a feeling of hope. Like biblical prophets, they hold out irrepressible hope that life is not necessarily preordained toward defeat, collapse, and tragedy, that fate is conquerable.

Such is the role and attraction of Francis, a gospel comedian! Peter Berger asserts that humor is a revelation of the transcendent, a cautious call to redemption, and for this reason "the actions of a clown take on a sacramental dignity."[81] This is what Saint Paul is referring to when he describes to the divisive Corinthians his own role as a clown of Christ, without social status and power: "We are fools for the sake of Christ, but you are wise. . . . We are weak, but you are strong. You are held in honor, but we in disrepute. . . . We have become like rubbish of the world, the dregs of all things, to this very day" (1 Cor 4:10, 13). All this means, of course, that Francis has become a ritual mourner in the church. By his words and actions he is allowing the people of God to name the grief that has been suppressing them for several decades, to relinquish it, and to be open to the new in hope. People have ceased to look over their shoulders to see if the "temple police" are watching, ready to insist that the rules be kept in every detail. With an immense relief people feel they can again dream that the mythology of Vatican II may at last become deeply embedded in the church.

---

[81] Peter Berger, *A Rumour of Angels: Modern Society and the Rediscovery of the Supernatural* (Harmondsmith: Penguin, 1969), 114.

Theological Reflection:
Personal and Corporate Discernment

Christ summons the Church as she goes her pilgrim way . . . to that continual reformation of which she always has need, in so far as she is a human institution here on earth.

—VATICAN II, *DECREE ON ECUMENISM*

A theology—and not simply a pastoral theology—which is in dialogue with other sciences and human experiences is most important for our discernment on how best to bring the Gospel message to different cultural contexts and groups.

—POPE FRANCIS, *EVANGELII GAUDIUM*

Saint John called us to personal and corporate discernment: "test the spirits to see whether they are from God" (1 John 4:1). Every time in history the institutional church forgets this imperative it sinks into cultural trauma because it has lost the willingness to follow John's imperative to be alert to what is or is not of God. Therefore, it is not surprising that when Saint Ignatius of Loyola founded his congregation of Jesuits in 1539 to reform the church, in the midst of the cultural trauma of ecclesiastical corruption and the Protestant Reformation, he insisted that this faith-inspired discernment, together with the *Spiritual Exercises,* should be at the heart of the Jesuit's and congregation's apostolic endeavors. Nor should we be surprised to find that Pope Francis has frequently referred to the essential role of discernment in evangelization (*EG,* nos. 33, 43, 50, 133). Through a faith-inspired discernment process we are called to identify within ourselves and the cultures in which we live what is or is not of the Spirit: "The wisdom of discernment redeems the necessary ambiguity of life and helps us find the most appropriate means, which do not always coincide with what looks great and strong."[82] The emphasis that Ignatius gave to the *Spiritual Exercises* and to discernment is as relevant today as it was in his time. We face the same challenge: the reform of the church.

Saint Ignatius's *Spiritual Exercises* are designed to train soldiers of Christ, but with a sensitivity to individual talents and needs. Thus they are suitable for people of all ages and cultures wishing to come closer to Christ and to serve his mission in the world. Ignatius urged that the *Exercises* "be adapted to the requirements of the persons who wish to make them . . . according to their age, their education, and their aptitudes." The *Exercises* are shaped to assist followers of Christ to make a choice in life at any stage of their lifecycle. This means abandoning whatever is not according to the will of God: "I must consider only the end for which I am created, that is, for the praise of God our Lord and for the salvation of my soul." The follower prays for "an intimate knowledge of the many blessings received, that filled with gratitude for all, [they] may in all things love and serve the Divine Majesty."[83] The apposite response for followers, no matter what age they are, is the prayer of Ignatius:

Take, Lord, and receive all my liberty, my memory, my understanding, and my entire will, all that I have and

---

[82] Pope Francis, in Spadaro, "A Big Heart Open to God."

[83] Ignatius of Loyola, *Spiritual Exercises,* ed. Louis J. Puhl (Chicago: Loyola University Press, 1951), nos. 18, 169, 234; see also no. 72.

possess. Thou has given all to me. To Thee, O Lord, I
return it. All is Thine, dispose of it wholly according
to Thy will. Give me Thy love and Thy grace, for this
is sufficient for me.[84]

This is a prayer of letting go, or of holy indifference. It is
the disciplined willingness to be detached from all that
hinders people from wholeheartedly serving Christ with
"a complete indifference with regard to created things, not
preferring health to sickness, riches to poverty, honor to
humiliation, long life to a short one. We wish only for those
conditions that will aid our pursuit of the goal for which we
were created."[85]

Ignatius described the ways in which this choice is to be
made by people who are motivated by holy indifference. The
first is the simplest method: when a person is able to choose
"without hesitation, or the possibility of hesitation."[86] The
second way is through scrutinizing the "experience of desola-
tions and consolations and discernment of spirits." Spiritual
consolation is where love is present. It is "an interior experience of the movement of the affections outward to other
human persons, the whole of humanity, to the communion
of saints, Christ and the Trinity, painful as that might be at
times."[87] Spiritual desolation is the darkness of the soul, a
time of significant temptation, and it is not the occasion
for making decisions about one's life. There is nothing
magical about discernment. It demands of individuals, and

---

[84] Ibid., no. 234.
[85] Ibid., no. 23.
[86] Ibid., no. 176.
[87] John English, *Spiritual Intimacy and Community: An Ignatian View
of the Small Faith Community* (London: Darton, Longman, and Todd,
1992), 50.

in corporate discernment of all members of the group, a profound faith in God and commitment to prayer, penance, and self-examination. Participants must also be willing to discover all possible information that relates to the issues that concern the individual or group. The third way of formulating a life's choice is during a time of tranquility in which a person ponders the purpose for which he or she has been created, the praise and glory of God and the person's salvation, and makes the choice in line with this end.[88]

In brief, the spirituality of Ignatius is deeply rooted in the scriptures, ultimately in the scriptural call to abandon all that is personally and institutionally holding us back from union with Christ Jesus and his mission. It is based on God's creative presence, not just in past actions, but in the events of everyday life. Consequently, we are called to search for God in all things. The more we are attuned to this presence of God the greater our happiness "even in the midst of a world of sorrow and pain."[89] This is authentic wisdom. Where God is not present—for example, in business relations, cultures of health and care facilities for the elderly, conditions that oppress people who are poor, unreformed ecclesiastical structures and attitudes—we are called to mediate Christ's presence through love, justice, and peace.[90]

Summary

- The Roman Curia was primarily responsible for embedding the conciliar mythology, but because it remained

---

[88] See Ignatius, *Spiritual Exercises,* no. 177.

[89] William A. Barry, *Spiritual Direction and the Encounter with God* (New York: Paulist Press, 1992), 78.

[90] See Susan Rakoczy, *Great Mystics and Social Justice* (New York: Paulist Press, 2006), 43–69.

unreformed the residual pre-conciliar mythology increasingly resurfaced. Censure and coercion forced people to grieve privately about this retreat from Vatican II; public mourning through responsible dissent was forbidden.

- Beginning about 2000 the suppressed grieving intensified as a result of the increasing revelations of abuse scandals, the continued insistence that pre-conciliar mythology be accepted, scapegoating within the church, and the bureaucratic dysfunctionalities within the Vatican. The grief reached overload proportions. Many symptoms of cultural trauma and impasse became evident: cynicism, fatalism, stagnation, widespread withdrawal from the church. In returning to the pre-conciliar mythology the church had ceased to be accountable for its actions on serious issues. What business consultant Peter Drucker says of secular organizations applies equally to the managerial poverty of the church at this time: "Any government, whether that of a company or of a nation, degenerates into mediocrity and malperformance if it is not clearly accountable for results and not clearly accountable to someone."[91]

- In the history of the church, even when morale and morality were at their lowest, movements of reform eventually arose "to animate and quicken its spirit."[92] Pope Francis by his actions and words is breaking through years of scandals, cultural trauma, and impasse, allowing the people of God to mourn openly and to hope for newness based on the mythology of Vatican II. As a ritual leader of mourning he is refounding

---

[91] Peter Drucker, *Post-Capitalist Society* (New York: HarperBusiness, 1993), 71.

[92] Jeffrey B. Russell, *A History of Medieval Christianity: Prophecy and Order* (New York: Thomas Y. Crowell, 1968), 99.

the church, seeking to draw others to join him in this collaborative process.

- Francis is alive to the dangers and weaknesses of being a charismatic figure. He knows that structures must be set firmly in place to allow the euphoria he is evoking in the people of God to become soundly institutionalized. Pope Adrian VI declared in 1523 that "we know well that even in this Holy See . . . abominable things have happened. . . . We intend to use all diligence to reform the Roman Curia."[93] A similar challenge now faces Francis. He must translate his symbolic gestures into wider structurally supported action at key levels of the church.

- An anthropologist cannot minimize the enormity of the challenges and risks confronting Francis. We need to be ever mindful of this anthropological axiom: *When strategies hit cultures, cultures win!* We cannot underestimate the built-in cultural resistances to reform within the church. Restorationism, with its roots firmly in pre-conciliar mythology, is very likely to go underground and remain a powerful residual mythology just waiting for the chance to resurface as it did after Vatican II. Francis is conscious of this danger. Already he has made changes to the curia, but he is aware that culture change is a slow process; discernment "takes time. . . . I believe that we always need time to lay the foundations for real, effective change. . . . I am wary of decisions made hastily."[94]

---

[93] Adrian VI, cited in Luigi Accattoli, *When a Pope Asks for Forgiveness* (New York: Alba House, 1998), 7.

[94] Francis, quoted in Spadaro, "A Big Heart Open to God."

7

From Mourning to Joy

The Ministry of Leadership

Let sorrow lend me words, and words express
The manner of my pity-wanting pain.
—WILLIAM SHAKESPEARE, "SONNET 111"

Blessed are those who mourn, for they will
be comforted.
—MATTHEW 5:4

Key points covered in this chapter

- For faith-focused people the scriptures provide the foundation for rituals of mourning and describe the qualities required in ritual leaders.
- The first quality of ritual leaders is that they themselves are able to mourn their own faults, in union with Christ the Mourner, thus becoming transformed by the vision of "the new heavens and the new earth, where righteousness is at home" (2 Pet 3:13); without this quality a ritual leader lacks compassion and empathy.

This chapter focuses on the scriptural foundations for rituals of mourning and on the role and qualities of ritual leaders. A basic theme of this book is that if people or cultures fail to process their grief—for example, in the closure of a valued school, parish, or hospital—through the tripartite stages of mourning rituals, the "suppressed tensions will in the end prove more profoundly disruptive than the social conflicts which relieve them."[1] If, however, appropriate rituals do occur, then within people's o'er-fraught hearts there is hope that many will begin to experience the joy of inner peace and embrace the future in hope.[2] The ultimate source of this inner peace is that mourners rediscover they already belong, however imperfectly, to Christ's promised kingdom through the life, death, and resurrection of Christ.[3]

There are various types of ritual leaders of mourning: those who lead secular change, such as CEOs of companies; and those called to lead change in faith-based organizations, such as bishops, pastors, and CEOs of ministries such as Catholic hospitals and schools. These people are formal

---

[1] Peter Marris, *Loss and Change* (London: Routledge and Kegan Paul, 1974), 91, 103.

[2] In the scriptures joy expressed in audible laughter is exceptional. We find, however, people who contemplate the many acts of divine humor and seek to mirror this humor in their own lives. This evokes inner joy, or what I term "laughter of the heart," coming from their faith in God's paradoxical love for them and humankind. See Gerald A. Arbuckle, *Laughing with God: Humor, Culture, and Transformation* (Collegeville, MN: Liturgical Press, 2008), 27–32.

[3] John Bowlby, "adapting a definition given by Anna Freud," sees healthy mourning occurring when an individual (or organization) is able "to accept both that a change has occurred in his external world and that he is required to make corresponding changes in his internal representational world and to reorganize, and perhaps to reorient, his attachment behavior accordingly." John Bowlby, *Loss: Sadness and Depression* (New York: Basic Books, 1980), 18 and 18n10.

ritual leaders because they are officially assigned to this task.[4] Informal ritual leaders are not publicly appointed to the task of leading mourning, but they have the personal gift of being able to call people to relinquish whatever is holding them back from authentic change.[5] For example, a person who listens empathetically to the grief of a bereaved person is an informal ritual leader.

Scriptural Examples: Ritual Mourners

Moses and Joshua

> When Moses told these words to all the
> Israelites, the people mourned greatly.
> —NUMBERS 14:39

Among the Israelites from time to time, in vivid contrast to their frequent experience of personal and corporate distress and grief, there are eruptions of surprising, even dramatic, newness or joy in the midst of grieving. The three stages of mourning—separation, liminality, and reentry (see Chapter 4)—are identifiable in these experiences. For the

---

[4] See Victor Turner, *The Drums of Affliction: Aspects of Ndembu Ritual* (Oxford: Clarendon Press, 1968), 1–8; Cecil G. Helman, *Culture, Health, and Illness* (Oxford: Butterworth-Heinemann, 1990), 192–93; Catherine Bell, *Ritual Theory, Ritual Practices* (New York: Oxford University Press, 1992), 130–40. Christen Lane defines formal ritual leaders as "those who devise new, or adapt old, rituals in order to uphold their definition of social relationships" (*The Rites of Rulers* [Cambridge: Cambridge University Press, 1981], 14).

[5] Formal ritual leaders are more common in stratified cultural groups in which there is a well-defined social hierarchy. Where this is not the case, informal ritual leaders flourish. See Mary Douglas, *Natural Symbols: Explorations in Cosmology* (New York: Pantheon Books, 1970), 86–87.

Israelites the period in the wilderness, after leaving Egypt and before becoming a bonded people (Exod 16—18), is the archetypal event of mourning in which Moses acts as God's exemplary formal ritual leader.

Moses followed the three-stage pattern of mourning with appropriate symbols and rituals at each phase. He acknowledged the importance of the separation period in which people journeyed out of Egypt, led by God in a pillar of cloud by day and fire by night, rejoicing that they are at last escaping oppression (Exod 1:17–22). Like all separation stages in mourning rituals this phase for the Israelites is filled with dramatic events, such as their escape through the sea and the destruction of the Egyptian army (Exod 14).

In the liminality stage they felt the pain of leaving the old and familiar world behind; there was hurting, anger, the desire to blame others for their misery: "Was it because there are no graves in Egypt that you have taken us away to die in the wilderness? What have you done for us, bringing us out of Egypt? . . . For it would have been better for us to serve the Egyptians than to die in the desert" (Exod 14:11–12). They are tempted to embrace pagan gods (Exod 32:1). They bicker and fight among themselves, become weary and lost. Moses keeps them, however, on the task of letting go their false attachments: "But Moses said to the people, 'Do not be afraid, stand firm, and see the deliverance that the Lord will accomplish for you today; for the Egyptians whom you see today you shall never see again. The Lord will fight for you, and you have only to keep still'" (Exod 14:13).

The reentry stage of the ritual is described in the book of Joshua. It portrays the entrance by the Israelites into the promised land after Moses had died and its partition among the twelve tribes under the official ritual leadership of Joshua. Joshua confronts the Israelites with their forgetfulness of God. They must relearn the lesson of their liminality stage in the desert: "If you forsake the Lord and serve foreign gods, then he will turn and do you harm, and consume you, after having done you good" (Josh 24:20). The people admit their faults: "For it is the Lord our God who brought us and our ancestors up from the land of Egypt, out of the house of slavery. . . . Therefore we also will serve the Lord, for he is our God" (Josh 24:17–18).[6]

God as Mourner

God, through Jeremiah, is described as a ritual leader united with the Israelites in their painful exile and calling them to put aside their false attachments. Their loss is God's loss. "My joy is gone, grief is upon me, my heart is sick. . . . For the hurt of my poor people I am hurt, I mourn, and dismay has taken hold of me" (Jer 8:18, 21). God feels the anguish of his people's loss, yet in the midst of the sorrow the new is already being dreamed about: "See, today, I appoint you over the nations . . . to pluck up and pull down . . . to build and to plant" (Jer 1:10). A radically new people will emerge from the chaos, provided they unite themselves with God's ritual of mourning and admit that without God they are powerless.

New Testament: Jesus Christ

Jesus is the master of creating mourning rituals. The dynamic of acknowledging dying and death, letting go and resurrection, is evident in much of the personal life and teaching methods of Jesus. His followers must learn the art of ongoing mourning, with its tripartite states, if they are to embrace the resurrection and lead other believers

---

[6] See Arbuckle, *Laughing with God*, 60–61.

appropriately. Ponder just a few examples. The first stage of mourning in the transfiguration incident[7] is when Jesus takes "Peter and John and James, and went up on the mountain to pray" (Luke 9:28). This is followed by the liminal phase, the confrontation with chaos, which includes the dramatic change in Jesus' appearance and the presence of Moses and Elijah who "appeared in glory" (v. 31). Peter and his companions wake up, and Peter's fear is evident in his attempt to control the thoroughly unpredictable through a flow of quite ridiculous speech and plans "to make three dwellings" (v. 33). Peter just has to impose order on the chaos that is frightening him, but the Father has other ideas for the three startled companions. They must be instructed to let go of Moses and Elijah, the pivotal symbols of the old covenant, if they are to embrace the newness of the new covenant in Christ. The two Old Testament figures disappear from sight, and "Jesus was found alone" (v. 36). They descend the mountain, filled with the inspiring experience, but they are slow to learn the lesson, so Jesus must continue to instruct them in the art of letting go of the old in order in order to embrace the new covenant.

The agony in the Garden of Gethsemane is for Jesus a drama of mourning that anticipates his ultimate ritual of mourning, namely, his death and resurrection.[8] Jesus is both that which is mourned and the ritual leader at the same time. The first stage of the ritual is the actual entrance of Jesus into the garden, symbolizing that some important ritual event is to begin. The liminality stage is characterized by reactions of fear, anxiety, and numbness when facing actual or anticipated loss. After the example of the lament

---

[7] Ibid., 76–78.

[8] See Gerald A. Arbuckle, *Change, Grief, and Renewal in the Church: A Spirituality for a New Era* (Westminster, MD: Christian Classics, 1991), 97–102.

psalms, Jesus does not camouflage or deny the sufferings
he is to experience in the liminal stage of the ritual. Thus
Mark records that as Jesus begins to pray he started "to be
distressed and agitated" (14:33), but the English translation
simply cannot convey the power of the Greek text. Words
such as horrified, shocked, or desolated are still too weak
to grasp what Mark is trying to say. Luke also highlights the
intensity of the agony of Jesus when he describes him praying with such earnestness that "his sweat became like great
drops of blood falling down on the ground" (Luke 22:44).
A little later Jesus describes it as "the power of darkness"
overwhelming him (Luke 22:53).The dramatic nature of
the emotional reaction to the anticipated grief is further
accentuated by the fact that, when Jesus foretold his death
previously, only the disciples had expressed anxiety and
desolation. Peter rebuked Jesus for thinking of his coming
death. The response of Jesus is filled with self-confidence,
no hint of sadness: "Get behind me, Satan! For you are set-
ting your mind not on divine things but on human things"
(Mark 8:33). But now, in Gethsemane, Jesus confronts the
harsh reality of his imminent scourging and death. This
evokes in him the strong emotions of horror, fear, and
temptation to flee the anguish. Jesus experiences the abso-
lute loneliness of his grief so poignantly described by the
psalmist: "There is no one who takes notice of me; no refuge
remains to me; no one cares for me" (Ps 142:4).

It is not only the anticipation of his sufferings and death
that cause him distress. The loss of innocence of the world
through sin and the way this alienates humankind from the
loving concern of the Father weigh heavily upon him. He
recognizes with more clarity than before the meaning of
his mission of loving obedience to the Father and what it
will cost him personally. An additional cause of his despondency is the failure of the disciples to remain empathetically

alert and at prayer with him in his time of need. Three times he goes to them to revive the support of their friendship. But they fail him. They remain asleep, uninterested in the pain of his journey and grieving. Peter is admonished by Jesus, especially because a short time before he had proudly boasted that "even though all become deserters, I will not" (Mark 14:29). He who was so prepared to die for Jesus lacks the strength at the crucial moment to watch one hour with him. Jesus reminds Peter that the Father offers him the grace of detachment so that he can be of service to his master in his hour of need. Peter must decide between this gift and his attachments to the familiar world of order. He chooses the latter and once more fails to mourn or to risk letting go, in hope, of his own security (Mark 14:37–41).

Finally, in the midst of the loneliness and darkness, Jesus cries out to the Father with a vigorous hope that he will intervene to help him. The spirit of detachment, integral to all authentic mourning, remains throughout the text: "Father, if you are willing, remove this cup from me; yet, not my will but yours be done" (Luke 22:42). Having prayed and allowed the old comforting security of companionship to go, Jesus is strengthened with new life to accept in a fully conscious way his death for the sins of the world. Now Jesus encounters a freshness and vitality in his actions that contrast markedly with his earlier dreads. It is a surprising newness that can only have its source in the Father. He knows what the Father wishes of him, and he now has the inner strength to do it, so he commands his sleeping followers to wake up and come with him to face his betrayal. Freshly energized, Jesus on his own initiative informs his captors-to-be that he is the one they want: "Then Jesus, knowing all that was to happen to him, came forward and asked them: 'Whom are you looking for?' They answered, 'Jesus of Nazareth.' Jesus replied, 'I am he'" (John 18:4–5). This confident movement by Jesus out of the liminal turmoil of the garden forms the third stage of his ritual of letting go. Fear remains, but it is now controlled by hope.

On the road to Emmaus the two disciples mirror the sadness of the wider community of disciples (Luke 24:13–25). Their journey predictably has the three stages of mourning, and Jesus acts engagingly as a ritual leader. The separation stage occurs when the companions freely and breathlessly express their grief to Jesus with anger and bewilderment because things have not turned out as they had desired: Jesus, their hoped-for revolutionary leader against the Roman oppressors, is dead. They then enter the liminality stage of their ritual mourning, and here Jesus, having won their trust, recounts the founding story of their salvation and strongly challenges them to recognize and accept their loss. This will open them to a community and personal newness beyond human imagination as a result of Jesus' death and resurrection (Luke 24:25–32). On interiorizing this message they experience a dramatic experience of hope, expressed by the words: "Were not our hearts burning within us?" (Luke 24:32). Immediately they want to share their joy with others. This is the reentry stage: "That same hour they got up and returned to Jerusalem" where "they told what had happened on the road" (Luke 24:33, 35).[9]

Gospel Ritual Leaders: Particular Qualities

Acknowledge Loss

The acknowledgment of loss by a ritual leader gives permission and encouragement to people to mourn publicly.

---

[9] See Arbuckle, *Laughing with God*, 86–87.

For example, in the Old Testament there are frequent and poignant calls to the people by the prophets to name their sorrows over a multitude of personal and national losses. God made a covenant with the people corporately so that when they experience the desolation of loss as a whole they need to mourn as a whole. If they mourn with converting hearts, then, God willing, the nation will relive the recreating power of the Exodus, the time when God first freely formed them out of nothing.[10] Following the example of the prophets and Jesus Christ, Pope Francis readily acknowledges the grief within the people of God: "It is undeniable that many people feel disillusioned and no longer identify with the Catholic tradition." He then indicates some of the causes of grief: "lack of pastoral care among the poor; the failure of our institutions to be welcoming. . . . Excessive centralization, rather than proving helpful, complicates the Church's life and her missionary outreach" (*Evangelii gaudium*, nos. 70, 32). At a more personal level, when asked, "Who is Jorge Mario Bergoglio?" he replied: "I am a sinner. This is the most accurate definition. It is not a figure of speech, a literary genre. I am a sinner."[11] He mourns that he is a sinner and in constant need of God's loving forgiveness and compassion. His admission encourages the people of God to likewise mourn.

Be a Self-Mourner

Authentic ritual leaders of mourning in a true sense are not *doers* of ritual but are *themselves* the ritual. They

---

[10] See Arbuckle, *Change, Grief, and Renewal in the Church*, 82.

[11] Antonio Spadaro, SJ, "A Big Heart Open to God," interview with Pope Francis, *America* (September 30, 2013), www.americamagazine.org/pope-interview.

make concrete by their inner conversion and conviction the idea that a new world is possible. Myth specialist Joseph Campbell describes a "hero" as one who "ventures forth from the world of common day into a region of supernatural wonder: fabulous forces are encountered and a decisive victory is won. The hero comes back from his mysterious adventure with the power to bestow boons on his fellow man."[12] He could be describing the qualities of the ritual leader. The ritual leader is a hero who has visited, and been converted to, the vision of a new world, and the ritual leader's behavior mirrors this interior transformation.

Thus, although ritual leaders need the appropriate human qualities, their preeminent skill must be their ability to mourn their own faults in union with Christ the Mourner, thus becoming transformed by the vision of the "new heavens and a new earth, where righteousness is at home" (2 Pet 3:13). They yearn to draw others to share this same dream in hope. Having been pilgrims on the journey of conversion, they know its dangers and the qualities that pilgrims need to survive, grow, and eventually lead others in mourning rituals. Unless one is able to mourn compassionately one's own failings and losses and so experience inner healing, it will be impossible to have empathy for the grief of others. Moses could never have kept to the role of ritual leader if he was not at the same time grappling with his own inner journey of faith and conversion. A naturally impatient man with a powerful temper (Exod 2:12; 32:19), he could not have survived without constantly praying to God out of the anguish of his own inner chaos.

---

[12] Joseph Campbell, *The Hero with a Thousand Faces* (Princeton, NJ: Princeton University Press, 1949), 30.

Be Listeners

Moses, like the other prophets, is open both to hearing God speaking to him and to recognizing the people's sufferings. He keeps contact with people by wandering around the camps and speaking informally to them outside their tents.[13] Christ's ministry is one of listening, both to the Father and to people. Their pain is his pain. On one occasion, as Jesus approaches Jerusalem, he pauses and looks out over the city, breaking into a powerful lament: "Jerusalem, Jerusalem. . . . How often have I desired to gather your children together as a hen gathers her brood under her wings, and you were not willing!" (Matt 23:37). The city's official leaders decline to lead the city in a lament for their failings and sins (Luke 19:39–40). Jesus knows that the city is to be destroyed after his death, so he mourns, openly weeping about the calamity: "They will crush you to the ground . . . and they will not leave within you one stone upon another; because you did not recognize the time of your visitation from God" (Luke 19:44).

Two qualities of listening must be emphasized: listening as hospitality and as healing. True hospitality offers people the space to feel free to unburden themselves, to clarify what is holding them back from moving forward. "Hospitality," writes Henri Nouwen, "is not a subtle invitation to adopt the lifestyle of the host, but the gift of a chance for the guest to find his own."[14] Listening is also healing, which is intimately connected to hospitality: "Healing means, first of all, the creation of an empty but friendly space where those who suffer can tell their story to someone who can listen with real attention."[15] Of course, true listening assumes

---

[13] See Arbuckle, *Change, Grief, and Renewal in the Church*, 151–56.
[14] Henri Nouwen, *Reaching Out* (London: Collins, 1976), 69.
[15] Ibid., 88.

a deep respect and concern for people. It means an unwillingness to offer solutions until the issues worrying people are fully listened to and heard. The supreme exemplar of these qualities of hospitality and healing is Christ. Ponder the many instances when he listened to the sufferings of people on the margins of society such as the lepers, the blind, the bereaved. He heard, and they left their distress behind and moved forward to new lives. The gift of listening is not something to be confined to formal ritual leaders such as qualified counselors and pastors; all are called at least to the ministry of informal ritual leadership. For example, travelers may be called to listen to the anguish of a stranger sitting beside them, and in the process, no matter how brief, there is a healing.

Be Open to Receive

Hospitality is not only about creating the space for others to be themselves, but it also involves an openness to receive as hosts from those who are our guests. Mutuality is at the heart of hospitality—a crucial lesson for formal and informal ritual leaders of mourning. This is evident in the life of Christ. For example, a centurion begs Jesus to heal his valued slave, but feeling unworthy to have Jesus in his house he asks that Jesus heal the sick man from a distance. Jesus is so deeply touched and amazed at the faith of the foreigner that he proclaims: "I tell you that not even in Israel have I found such faith" (Luke 7:9). The act of healing is a formal ritual of mourning. The man is freed from his sickness and is able to return to his task as a beloved servant of the centurion, but Jesus receives in return the joy of discovering the faith of the centurion. I see this same dynamic eminently present in L'Arche communities. At the heart of these communities are people with intellectual disabilities, and for this reason they are called core persons; those who care for them are termed assistants. Core people are so named because they are the primary teachers in their communities. While assistants provide the security and space for core people to be themselves, the assistants repeatedly tell me that in return they receive so much—reminders that we all are ultimately fragile people in need of love and respect.

Do Not Rush Liminality

Working through grief may not have a definite time limit set upon it. This will often depend on the depth of grief being suffered by individuals and cultures. Hence, ritual leaders must resist the desire to cut short the liminality or chaos stage. It is there that participants have to grapple with the chaos and gradually work through the tension between the desire to remain attached to the past and the openness to the new. Thus Moses was sensitive to the need to allow ample time for the Israelites to let go the past and to be open to the vision of the promised land (Deut 8:2, 3, 5).

Jesus knew that one experience of liminality for the disciples would never be sufficient. To be one with Jesus, his disciples, always slow to understand, often had to be given ample room to grapple with their own exodus experiences. So the liminality of the desert or wilderness theme was frequently to the fore in Christ's life and in his teaching of his disciples.[16] His call to his apostles came in a wilderness place, and he drew them back there wherever he wished to teach them matters of critical importance (Mark 6:31–32). Thus, "Jesus took with him Peter and James and John, and

---

[16] See Augustine Stock, *The Way in the Wilderness: Exodus, Wilderness, and Moses Themes in Old Testament and New* (Collegeville, MN: Liturgical Press, 1969), 68–69.

led them up a high mountain apart, by themselves" to experience his divinity (Mark 9:2-7). He allowed the apostles to be terrified by a storm on a lake in order to teach them in the midst of the liminal experience the meaning of faith (Mark:39-40). However, both Moses and Jesus Christ, while not rushing the liminality stage in their mourning rituals, recognized the need for its closure and movement forward into the reentry stage. Chronic mourning must be avoided.

Respect the Power of Silences

Sit in silence, and go into darkness.
—Isaiah 46:5

I remember an inspiring Maori chief, Waimarama Puhara, whom I knew when I was a small boy in New Zealand. When acting as the tribal ritual leader in mourning he would often pause before the people in total silence. A hush would descend on those present, no one feeling uncomfortable with the silences. He realized that at times nonverbal communication in mourning can be far more powerful than words. There is the scene where Jesus is before the council, falsely indicted by the conflicting testimony of his accusers. When it is obvious that people are lying, "the high priest stood up before them and asked Jesus, 'Have you no answer?'" (Mark 14:60). Instead of replying verbally, Jesus "was silent and did not answer" (Mark 14:61). By his silence—a ritual liminal space—Jesus was calling the high priest and his followers to mourn the loss of their integrity. Words would have distracted them, but the silence urged them to confront their mendacity. But they refused to accept the challenge.

Be Prophetic

The prophets are courageous people, risking at times even death in order to call people to lament their waywardness. Jeremiah, for example, stands in the Old Testament as a lonely, tragic person, but he has the skill of using ritual mourning as a way of confronting the Israelites with their rebellious ways. They must return to their covenant obligations or face the death of their culture and nation. But his message is immensely costly to him. Ponder a little one of the prophet's personal laments (Jer 15:10–21). He vents his anger against God, describing the abuse he suffers because of his ritual role: "Truly, you are to me like a deceitful brook, like waters that fail" (Jer 15:18). But when Jeremiah laments his failures and God's apparent lack of gratitude to a loving companion, God immediately accepts his repentance. Jeremiah once again feels the revitalizing embrace of God in his prophetic task. The sensitive, hesitant prophet becomes once more "a fortified city, an iron pillar and a bronze wall, against the whole land" (Jer 1:18). A similar courage marks the behavior of Christ as he calls people to let the old covenant pass to allow the new to enter. At the beginning of this public ministry, while visiting his hometown, he boldly proclaims that he is the one sent by God to redeem Israel: "Today this scripture is being fulfilled in your hearing" (Luke 4:21). But the people would not assent to this. They "drove him out of the town . . . so that they might hurl him off the cliff" (Luke 4:29). At this point he avoided death, but it would eventually be the price he would pay for his courage in challenging people to mourn their defiant behavior.

We desperately need leaders, such as Pope Francis, who are able to create rituals by their lifestyle and actions, which challenge us to abandon our attachment to all that holds us back from personal and organizational transformation.

Prophetic people go to the heart of the gospel story, wisely discarding all accidental and historical accretions. They identify the gaps between the healing mission of Christ and the reality around them and, with imagination and courage, find ways to bridge those gaps through appropriate rituals of mourning. This is why mourning rituals are at the heart of refounding. In the midst of the turmoil in the church radical change will not be reenacted merely by superficially improving old failed methods of leadership. More radical responses are necessary in order to move forward.

Clarify Vision

In the midst of the people's mourning Moses rearticulates the visionary newness of the time ahead of them, "For the Lord your God is bringing you into a good land, a land with flowing streams . . . a land of wheat and barley" (Deut 8:7–8). He never hesitates to call the people to be accountable to this vision: "So be careful not to forget the covenant that the Lord your God made with you" (Deut 4:23). Jesus by word and action would repeatedly articulate the vision of the kingdom (Luke 6:20, 22–23) in direct language, parables, and action because his followers were "slow of heart to believe all that the prophets have declared" (Luke 24:25). Dramatic experiences of liminality left even his special friends, Peter, James, and John, untouched in the depths of their hearts. The process of mourning is indeed slow!

Need to Maintain Roots

Moses, in addition to reminding his people of the vision of the promised land ahead, appreciates their need to maintain contact with their collective cultural roots in Egypt during the liminality stage of mourning in the desert (Exod 8:7–8). He encourages them to collect the bones of their ancestor Joseph and to carry them into the wilderness (Exod 13:19).[17] Thus in the mergers of parishes, for example, people should carry some symbol(s) from their former parishes to the new parish center.

Call to Remember

Theologian Robert Schreiter wisely reminds us that "to urge the forgetting of painful memories and events is to either trivialize the events themselves . . . or to trivialize the victim (you are not significant enough to have been offended that much)." The forgetting to which we are called in rituals of mourning is "an overcoming of anger and resentment, a being freed from the entanglements of those emotions and their capacity to keep us bound to an event."[18] In the Old Testament, for example, the Israelites frequently are called to remember not just the pains of the chaos of the Exodus and the exile, but also their benefits. Moses reminds them: "Remember that you were a slave in the land of Egypt, and the Lord your God brought you out of there with a mighty hand and an outstretched arm" (Deut 5:15). Saint Paul also recalls his own sufferings, but then the joy of knowing Christ: "Remember Jesus Christ, raised from the dead. . . . That is my gospel, for which I suffer hardship. . . . But the word of God is not chained" (2 Tim 2:8–9).

---

[17] Psychologists speak of transitional objects; to lose symbols of attachment is to lose one's identity in the process of change.

[18] Robert Schreiter, *The Ministry of Reconciliation: Spirituality and Strategies* (Maryknoll, NY: Orbis Books, 2000), 66, 67.

Avoid Creating Dependency

In times of chaos people whose certitudes and sense of order have disintegrated are susceptible to manipulation by charismatic persons, who can use people for their own narcissistic advantage.[19] Aberrant charismatic ritual leaders may even twist sacred texts, to support their hold over their followers. Therefore, the task of a ritual leader, as exemplified in the ministries of Moses and Jesus, is to empower the people and cultures to assume responsibility for their own mourning. The ritual leader must resist the temptation to allow people to become overly dependent. Neither Moses nor Jesus succumbed to this temptation. As the ritual re-entry stage of mourning—the entrance into the promised land—is about to begin for the Israelites, Moses slips away, with remarkable detachment, to die alone on a mountain and to rest in an unmarked grave (Deut 32:1–7).

Jesus, like Moses before him, was at pains to avoid creating a dangerous and immature culture of dependency among his followers. Throughout his preaching Jesus concentrated on the mission of the Father (John 2:17) and the Spirit: "It is for your own advantage that I go away, for if I do not go away, the Advocate will not come to you" (John 16:7). After the crucifixion he resisted Mary Magdalen's yearning to cling to him: "Do not hold on to me, because I have not yet ascended to the Father. But go to my brothers and say to them: 'I am ascending to my Father and your Father; to my God and your God'" (John 20:17). At Emmaus, just when the two disciples are in danger of developing undue emotional dependency on their guest, Jesus disappears (Luke 24:31). They had to stand on their own as autonomous persons,

---

[19] See Charles Lindholm, *Charisma* (Oxford: Blackwell, 1993), 47.

owning the authority that they had received at their ritual of baptism and acting accordingly.[20]

Respect Dissenters

Responsible dissenters ritually call people to relinquish undue attachments. Organizations, to be effective, need people who feel free to dissent dutifully, even from formally appointed ritual leaders. There is a relevant example of this in the life of David, the official Israelite mourner. David laments the loss of his son Absalom: "The king covered his face, and the king cried with a loud voice, 'O my son Absalom, O Absalom, my son, my son'" (2 Sam 19:4). However, his grief becomes chronically protracted and threatens to undermine his leadership and the welfare of his soldiers and people. Joab, his friend, then decides to step in and remind David of his duties as a ritual leader. He bluntly tells David that the time of mourning is over and the future has to be faced constructively: "You have made it clear today that commanders and officers are nothing to you. . . . So go out at once and speak kindly to your servants; for I swear by the Lord, if you do not go, not a man will stay with you this night" (2 Sam 19:6, 8). David is brought back to reality and speedily does what he is asked and returns to his role as ritual leader: "Then the king got up and took his seat in the gate. The troops were told, 'See, the king is sitting in the gate'; and all the troops came before the king" (2 Sam 19:9). David then successfully leads his troops through the reentry stage of mourning (2 Sam 19:16).

---

[20] See Gerald A. Arbuckle, *From Chaos to Mission: Refounding Religious Life Formation* (Collegeville, MN: Liturgical Press, 1995), 200.

Appreciate the Role of Humor

Incongruity or paradox is at the heart of humor. It can allow people to relax, briefly put aside their feelings of loss, thus giving them the chance to reimagine alternative ways of acting. It can be a positive method of releasing tension and frustration.[21] Even today, among Australian Aboriginal peoples, who have been forced for generations to be second-class citizens in a country where they were the first owners, humor is a ritual way to cope with their feeling of marginalization.[22] Jesus also frequently uses humor in his lifestyle and parables, for example, because its subversive quality can deflate pomposity and undermine the rigidity of the status quo. The ultimate source of his humor is his detachment from self, his humility, and his total faith in the Father, evident in the mourning ritual of his life, death, and resurrection: "Who, though he was in the form of God . . . emptied himself, taking the form of a slave, being born in human likeness" (Phil 2:6–7).

Plan Rituals

Rituals of mourning need to be planned carefully. The more important and threatening the transition, the more formal and orderly the ritual. People need to feel that something vitally significant is to be enacted, but if the ritual is not well prepared, this sense of importance will not be present.

---

[21] See Arbuckle, *Laughing with God*, 13, 15–16.
[22] Ritual leaders among the Lodagaa people of West Africa deliberately cultivate laughter on the second day of funeral in order to moderate the grief of the bereaved. See Jack Goody, *Death, Property and the Ancestors: A Study of the Mortuary Customs of the Lodagaa of West Africa* (London: Tavistock Publications, 1962), 123.

People will feel that they themselves and their grief are being trivialized. Moses was sensitive to the fact that the experience of chaos in the Exodus, a precondition for forming a new people, if not guided prudently, could lead to total destruction. Therefore, he sought the advice of Jethro, his father-in-law, who instructed him to group the people into manageable administrative units under the direction of "men who fear God, are trustworthy, and hate dishonest gain" (Exod 19:21). Jethro bluntly told Moses that he needed time to pray in order to discover God's vision and plans for the people to abandon the past in order to move forward (Exod 18:19–20). He wisely heeded this advice.

A Mourning Ritual

The following mourning ritual has been used many times with groups as large as five hundred and as small as five. Its simplicity, the use of the biblical mourning loss and newness paradigm, and periods of meditative silence invariably provide participants with space in which they can name their losses, struggle to relinquish their hold over them, and move forward in hope.[23]

Preliminary Instructions
- As participants enter in silence into a darkened room, they are given a lighted candle and move into circles of eight (or fewer); the paschal candle is alight in the center of the room; meditative background music can be played.
- It is advisable not to extend the ritual beyond approximately one hour.

---

[23] This ritual, devised by Gerard Whiteford, SM, was first published in Gerald A. Arbuckle, *Refounding the Church: Dissent for Leadership* (Maryknoll, NY: Orbis Books, 1993), 197–98. It has been adapted for this publication.

- If the ritual is to be a community experience, then the ritual leader should be the officially appointed group leader, if possible.

Process

Leader:
- Reads Isaiah 45:7.
- Invites all to enter into the darkness of the tomb so that they may discover the newness of the resurrection.

Reader:
- Reads Psalm 143.

Leader:
- Invites all to ponder this question: What significant thing do I feel I have lost personally or communally?
- Pauses for a few moments.
- Invites participants to name some loss or grief that they have experienced, advising them to keep their naming to one word or a phrase. There is no discussion of what is named.
- After each participant names a loss, then the person extinguishes his or her candle.
- After all the participants have named a loss, the paschal candle and lights are extinguished.
- Meditative silence for a short period.

Reader:
- Reads Psalm 88.
- Meditative silence for a lengthy period.

Leader:
- Invites participants to identify in silence some newness or joy that has entered their personal life or their group's ministry.
- Lights the paschal candle.
- Meditative silence for a brief period.
- Invites people to name the newness they have experienced.
- Each participant, after naming a newness, lights his or her candle from the paschal candle.
- After all candles are lighted, there is a short period of meditative silence.

- Reads Revelation 21:1–7.
- Invites the group to sing together a resurrection hymn.
- Invites all to share the sign of peace.

Seek Forgiveness

To forgive is to abandon the anger and resentment felt in response to harm that is done. The condition for obtaining God's forgiveness for our sins is our willingness to forgive those who have hurt us or caused us loss (Mark 11:25). Ultimately, the test of one's love of God is one's willingness to do this (Luke 10:37; Matt 18:33). Admittedly, forgiving a person, a culture, a government, is extremely difficult, especially when the violator shows no remorse for the actions. Robert Schreiter helpfully explains that forgiveness is both a process and a decision.[24] An essential first part of the slow process is to recall and acknowledge the enormity of the personal or group loss that has occurred through the actions of others. It is in the liminality stage that people are invited and encouraged to forgive. The bereaved decides not to be controlled by the events and feelings of the past but to move forward to build a new future and identity. Forgiving does not mean condoning, excusing, or forgetting what has happened; it may be necessary to seek compensation and the appropriate reform of those who caused the harm. In brief, the past and its lessons are not to be forgotten, but their power to hold back the bereaved from moving forward is removed. When this happens, the bereaved may be reconciled to the violator, even when the perpetrator is refusing to apologize and to compensate for the wrongs done.

---

[24] See Schreiter, *The Ministry of Reconciliation*, 55–69.

John Lederach, a Mennonite Christian who has experience of peacebuilding in fractured societies, analyzes the relevance of Psalm 85:10 for our understanding of forgiveness.[25] The psalmist, Lederach explains, is describing the return of the exiled Israelites to their land and the chance for a new peace:

> Steadfast love and faithfulness will meet;
> righteousness and peace will kiss each other.

"Steadfast love" refers to recognizing what has happened together with its attendant pain and suffering; "faithfulness," to letting go of the past and being open to the future; "righteousness," to searching for individual and group rights to be upheld and due compensation to be granted; and "peace," to establishing unity and solidarity between the violated and the violators. The biblical process of forgiveness, therefore, is the ongoing struggle to keep these four qualities in balance.

Seek Professional Assistance

Ritual leaders must recognize their limitations. The process of mourning can be so tortuous for some people that professional assistance is necessary. In group mourning rituals, for example, not everyone can be expected to be at the same stage, and a ritual leader may not recognize this without professional help. Also, chronic or pathological grief requires that the ritual leader be highly skilled in the appropriate social sciences, such as psychology or psychiatry.

---

[25] See Jon Lederach, *Building Peace: Sustainable Reconciliation in Divided Societies* (Washington DC: Institute of Peace, 1997), 29.

If not, the ritual leader should direct individuals or groups to seek specialized assistance.

Summary

- Mourning rituals have a twofold function: to "provide the opportunity for a catharsis that releases the energy that has been invested in emotional repression,"[26] and to rearticulate a sense of purpose or meaning in people's lives. Both intuitive and instrumental mourners benefit from these functions, but in slightly different ways. The former particularly appreciate the chance for "affective ventilation," and the latter find the rituals help them focus their thoughts and aid them in "meaning making."[27]
- There must be ritual leaders gifted with the necessary spiritual and human gifts who can creatively develop appropriate rituals of mourning, because the process of mourning is an often extremely difficult and complex one.
- Many among the people of God are confused and justly angry with the failings and abuses of power in the church since Vatican II. They yearn for scripture-based rituals of mourning that allow their grief to

---

[26] David M. Noer, *Healing the Wounds: Overcoming the Trauma of Layoffs and Revitalizing Downsized Organizations* (San Francisco: Jossey-Bass, 1993), 92.

[27] Kenneth J. Doka and Terry L. Martin, *Grieving Beyond Gender: Understanding the Ways Men and Women Mourn* (New York: Routledge, 2010), 192. As we saw in Chapter 3, intuitive grief occurs when individuals and groups, according to Doka and Martin, "experience and express grief in an affective way"; instrumental grief is predominantly "experienced physically, such as in a restlessness or cognition" (ibid., 4).

speak publicly with the hope that they can at last move forward to build a church based on conciliar thinking.

- Prophetic people are ritual leaders of mourning in the church. By their lifestyle, actions, and words they confront a world of status, power manipulation, and corruption. They are without the power that the world applauds. Their powerlessness gives them the freedom to challenge the world they critique, for they ultimately depend on no one but Jesus Christ, whose words and actions model authentic mourning.[28]

---

[28] See Victor Turner, *The Ritual Process: Structure and Anti-Structure* (Ithaca, NY: Cornell University Press, 1977), 167–203.

Index